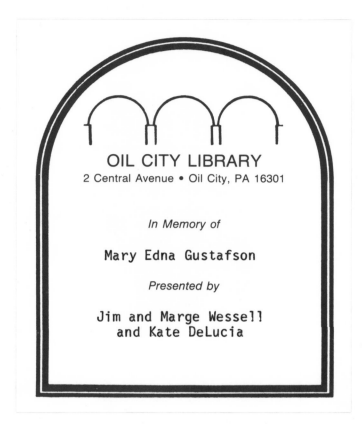

Quilting
with Style
Principles
for Great Pattern Design

Quilting
with Style
Principles
for Great Pattern Design

Gwen Marston &
Joe Cunningham

American Quilter's Society

P. O. Box 3290 • Paducah, KY 42002-3290

ALL PHOTOGRAPHS BY THE KEVA PARTNERSHIP, FLINT MICHIGAN, UNLESS OTHERWISE NOTED.

ALL ANTIQUE QUILTS SHOWN IN THIS BOOK ARE IN THE COLLECTION OF GWEN MARSTON.

Library of Congress Cataloging-in-Publication Data

Marston, Gwen.
     Quilting with style : principles for great pattern design / Gwen
Marston & Joe Cunningham.
          p.   cm.
     Includes bibliographical references and index.
     ISBN 0-89145-814-x : $24.95
          1. Quilting–Patterns–Design.   2. Patchwork–Patterns–Design.
3. Appliqué–Patterns–Design.   4. Quilting–Patterns.
5. Patchwork–Patterns.   6. Appliqué–Patterns.   I. Cunningham,
Joe.   II Title.
TT835.M37751993
746.9'7041–dc20   93–7673
                                                                    CIP

Additional copies of this book may be ordered from:

American Quilter's Society
P.O. Box 3290
Paducah, KY 42002-3290
@24.95. Add $1.00 for postage and handling.

Copyright: 1993, American Quilter's Society

THIS BOOK IS DEDICATED TO

UNKNOWN QUILTERS

OF THE PAST AND PRESENT.

PLATE 1. Bars, 78" x 78", 1986. Made by Gwen Marston.
This was a version of a quilt first shown in *The Pieced Quilt*, by Jonathan Holstein
(p. 97). All the quilting designs are typical of the Old Order Amish style: fancy feather
border, pumpkin seed on the narrow inner border, and crosshatching over the bars.
Making a "classical" quilt like this, Gwen thought she should stick with classic quilting.

TABLE OF CONTENTS

PLATE 2. Whig Rose, detail; full quilt shown on page 154.

INTRODUCTION

Quiltmaking has become a, seemingly, permanent part of our age. Quilts appear in newspapers, magazines, books, auction houses and museums. Quilt guilds continue to proliferate. Quilts are written about, studied, documented, and photographed by the thousands. Contests offer the chance for fame and cash to innumerable quilters here and abroad.

What excites most people about quilts is the unique effect of designs made with fabric. New or old, it is the unusual graphic quality of quilts that makes them resemble art, or, in the case of quilts by quilt artists, it is the graphic design that is the art. It seems that the least part of a quilt is the quilting. When quilters talk about "designing a quilt," they almost always mean the quilt top. The quilting is almost always considered a supplementary process, the purpose of which is to emphasize or deemphasize aspects of the graphic design of the top. Quilting has simply declined in importance since the time when it was as significant a part of the quilt as the piecing or appliqué.

There are a number of reasons for this. First, hand quilting, unlike piecing or appliqué, employs an unusual stitching technique. Most quiltmaking techniques are part of basic sewing. It is nearly as easy to learn piecing or appliqué from books as it would be to learn from one's grandmother. Quilting, however, is unlike other sewing. It is difficult – at best – to learn from a teacher, and extremely difficult to learn from books. Moreover, until this century, quilting was almost always done in a full-size frame – that huge, lumbering apparatus you might remember from a great-aunt's house. The frame required so much space and such an unusual stitching technique that many quilters had decided not to bother with it. Most modern quilters use the quilting hoop; others practice machine quilting or tying instead of tedious hand quilting.

Second, the invention and development of the polyester batt has made extensive quilting unnecessary. Unlike nineteenth-century cotton "wadding," polyester batting barely needs to be quilted at all. Whereas cotton needs to be quilted closely to prevent shifting and bunching, polyester will remain stable even if it is just tied with a knot every 12 inches.

Third are the commercial incentives to downplay hand quilting. They primarily have to do with time: the more hand quilting we do, the longer it will be before we need to buy more quilting products. Commercially, then, it makes sense to encourage as much small and quick work as possible.

Fourth, despite this age of efficiency and labor-saving machines, even if we want to do extensive hand quilting, it seems we all have less time to pursue that kind of activity. Most quilters of the past stayed at home all day, while many quilters today hold full-time jobs. There is no way to make hand quilting "quick and easy." One simply has to sit at the frame or hoop for a good number of hours and sew.

All of this is not to mention the fact that the quilting does not show from a distance. Unlike richly patterned piecing or appliqué that can be appreciated by the most casual of observers, quilting appeals more to the few who appreciate its subtle effects.

In spite of all this, quilting is our favorite part of the quiltmaking process. There is nothing we like better than sitting at the frame, quilting, talking, listening to music or enjoying the silence. When we see an old quilt, the first thing we study is the quilting.

Obviously, we feel that the quilting can be as significant a part of a quilt as its piecing or appliqué. At least, a lack of quilting does nothing to enhance a top. In general, we think almost any quilt top benefits when the quilting is taken seriously.

Because we have been unable to find the kind of information about quilting that we needed – how to draft quilting patterns, how to mark them, how to decide which ones to use and when to use them – we have had to work out techniques and methods for ourselves. Along the way we have filled dozens of files with our notes.

It is from those files that this book has been made. We cannot claim that our techniques for drafting cables are historical. We do not know for sure how heart designs used to be marked. All we know for sure is that all the designs in this book can be drafted, marked and quilted in the way we describe – because we have done it ourselves. While we have been writing this book, we have also continued to make quilts, and we have turned again and again to our notes on patterns.

When we started this project, our idea was to write the book that we had wished was available when we began making quilts. Throughout the text, we have emphasized that the lessons and instructions are meant to convey underlying concepts, not specific projects. In other words, what is important is not how to design a cable for a 3" border, but how to design a cable. Our aim is to cover thoroughly the most common traditional quilting designs. We will only be able to hint at the thousands of original variations and designs. After following the instructions you should be able to draft any of the patterns you want for your quilt. We do not want to teach you to make quilts like ours, but rather to give you the tools you need to make quilts you may have wanted to make but did not know how.

In other words, we wanted to write a sort of "cookbook" of quilting designs. Experienced cooks know that heating eggs and milk too quickly will make them curdle. Peeking at the rice before it is done will make it sticky. Tossing in the flour can make the gravy lumpy. These cooks don't need a recipe for most dishes because they understand the basic principles behind them.

Drafting quilting designs is like cooking. Once you see how the basic principles are combined and recombined, altered and improvised upon, you see that you don't really need a pattern for a particular quilting design – because you can cook up your own. You can double or halve the recipe according to the size of your guest blocks or borders.

There is nothing mysterious about making quilts. Our forbearers figured out for themselves what they needed to know to accomplish their quilts. With none of the advantages we have today, such as large libraries of quilt books, access to teachers, videos, and magazines, they nevertheless created the body of work that makes up the American quilt tradition. The advantage they did have was that they thought they could do it. They thought they could figure out for themselves how to solve problems in quiltmaking. This attitude led to unusual, sometimes bizarre, patterns and techniques that could only have been invented by someone who did not know that he/she could not do it. Today, if a quilter wants to know how to do something, she most often takes a class or buys a book.

We do not want to discourage you from taking classes or buying books. But we do want to remind you that there are many paths to the same goal. If you want to make quilts, the first tool you need is the knowledge that you can make them any way you like. Learn a few basic principles and you can go to work. When it comes to the quilting designs we hope this book will give you exactly those principles you need to go forward on your own.

CHAPTER 1

GETTING STARTED

PLATE 3. Rose Wreath, detail. Full quilt shown on page 35.

We often speak of "styles of quilts." And just as often we find that many quilters do not know exactly what we mean. Since the concept of "style" will be central to many of the ideas discussed later, we thought we should spend some time now discussing the subject.

IDENTIFYING QUILT STYLES

Perhaps the most widely-known style of quilts is the pre-1940 Old Order Amish style: all solid colors; simple medallion designs such as center diamonds, center squares, or bars, surrounded by narrow inner and wider outer borders. These are usually quilted in rich feathers, cross-hatchings, stars, and other such designs, usually with non-contrasting thread. Most quilters know an Old Order Amish quilt when they see one, even if they might be hard pressed to define just what makes them so sure.

Old Order Amish quilts have hall-marks, such as those listed above, but an Amish quilt is not a set of rules or a for-mula. Its style is evident in certain charac-teristics, but an Old Order Amish quilt does not consist of only those characteristics. The style is the result of a complex web of cultural and circumstan-tial factors that cannot be reproduced. So, unless you are Amish and travelling back fifty years in time, you cannot make an "Old Order Amish" quilt. What you *can* do is make a quilt in the Amish style. You can choose one of the typical patterns, such as a center diamond; use a typical color palette, such as red, purple, blue and green; and quilt the top with typical designs, such as feather wreaths, pump-kin seeds, crosshatching, and clamshells. Depending upon your faithfulness to details, such as color of thread, width of binding, backing material, etc., your quilt will be more or less "Amish" looking.

These elements that make up the style can be imitated. They can also be studied and appropriated individually, as many contemporary quiltmakers do when they make an original design using elements of the Amish style, such as an Amish color scheme. Within the Old Order Amish style, each community of quilters, and indeed each quilter herself, had an individual style. It was not something self-consciously developed and planned. Each person's style, the result of her unique life experiences, could be studied and imitated as well.

If you have made any quilts at all, you have already started to develop you own style. Certain kinds of patterns and colors probably appeal to you more than others. Perhaps quilts do not look "right" to you without a fairly wide border. Perhaps you like patterns that interlock and overlap, or prefer appliquéd floral patterns. Perhaps you copied a quilt from a book or magazine pattern but could not bring yourself to use the colors of the original.

If you continue to make quilts, you will develop a more or less distinctive style of your own, whether you mean to or not – just as every quilter of the past did. Being aware of other people's styles and becoming familiar with their elements can help you develop you own.

If, for instance, you wanted to make an old-fashioned quilt for an old-fashioned room, you could try to think about what an old-fashioned quilt would look like. Using enough imagination, you might be able to come up with a quilt that would look right in the room. Or, you could consider just how old-fashioned the room is. Let us say you have a fairly simple antique dresser with an old rope bed. This would put you somewhere around the middle of the nineteenth century, in a modest home. Knowing that, you could look at the everyday quilts of the mid-nineteenth century. You would find "chopped" corners on borders, instead of engineered, symmetrical ones. And you would find certain kinds of quilting, such as feather designs, certain kinds of straight-line fillers, certain kinds of floral quilting.

As we say, if you want to make a quilt that will be harmonious with the room,

you will want to study the style of the quilts being make when the furniture was made. Part of that style will be the quilting.

This does not apply only to historical periods. Modern quilts are often, though not always, made in the modern style. The quilting on modern quilts has its own hallmarks. Because of the current view of quilting as secondary to the graphic design, quilting lines today often echo the piecing with straight lines. Some quilters prefer to have flowing, curving lines like those often used to signify the wind, or waves. However, whether it uses straight lines or curved, modern quilting is almost always abstract, rarely pictorial.

You can learn a lot about styles of quilting just by looking at pictures of quilts in books. Pick a type of quilt, such as contemporary floral appliqués. Look at pictures of them. How are they quilted? How far apart are the straight lines? Does the quilting go over the appliqué or around it? Study a dozen or so quilts and you will become acquainted with some of the conventions. Try the same exercise with other styles, such as old red and green appliqués. Try it with quilts made in the 1930's. Soon you will have a feeling for a number of different styles, even if you can't define exactly what makes them up.

CHOOSING QUILTING DESIGNS

Chances are, this is not the only quilting book you have or have seen. If you are like most of us, you probably look at pictures of quilts or at quilts themselves and notice only the graphic design of the top. This is natural, as the design of the top is what stands out the most. In many photographs, the quilting is hard to see, even if you are looking for it. Many publications on the subject make us wonder why the objects are even called "quilts," when the quilting seems to be so thoroughly unimportant.

A revealing exercise is to return to some of your favorite quilt books and look at the pictures again. This time, ignore the patchwork – look only at the quilting. You might have to use a magnifying glass. When *we* do this it makes us feel as if we have two books in one. When we are trying to decide what to quilt, this is exactly what we do, and we are always surprised at the rich world of designs still to be found on quilts we have studied dozens of times before.

Quilters often ask us for advice on how to quilt particular tops, because they seem to have no feeling for which kinds of quilting might suit them or their quilts best. Before you can develop a feeling for this, you need to know what your options are: what kinds of quilting you like to look at, and what kinds you like to do, as well as what kinds of quilting are most practical with the techniques you use. Our first advice, then, is to develop a sense of your personal preferences. Just look at a lot of quilting and think about what you like best.

This seems simple because it is. But it is also important. Because quilting receives so little attention, quilters often feel helpless when the time comes to choose what to quilt, and this feeling of helplessness contributes to the anxiety that often unnecessarily surrounds the making of a quilt.

A system many use for choosing designs is the "default" system: you have a template you have purchased to use on another quilt top and it does not seem right to just throw it away. It is there, and you need a design, so you use it by default. Commercial templates have been around for at least a hundred and fifty years. Many new ones are very good – well made and beautiful. But a template designed for a 6" border should not be used on a 9" border just because it is handy. Nor should quilters decide to put 6" borders on their quilts because they have 6" quilting templates!

There is nothing inherently wrong with letting a template direct your work. But we prefer to have more flexibility with our quilts. It makes more sense to us to be free at every step of the way to use the technique or design for which the quilt seems to call.

We do not mean to disparage the use of commercial templates, only the *misuse* of them. Commercial templates may be just what you need for rare patterns, or for designs that are difficult to draft to the exact size you need. Anything that increases your options is good and helpful.

If you have a quilt top you are wondering how to quilt, the place to start looking is the top itself. Does it have large areas of plain fabric? If so, then the quilting can play a major role in the finished piece. Is it densely pieced with few or no plain areas? Then the quilting will probably play a supporting role. Is it in the Pennsylvania German style, with bold reds, yellows, and greens? Then you may want to use designs based on those found on the originals, such as hearts, pineapples, cables, and feathers. Is it Amish in style? Study Amish quilts of the same or similar pattern. Is it a more modern quilt top, intended primarily as art? Perhaps you will want to use designs typical of modern art quilts: straight line variations of the pieced pattern, flowing wind-like lines, or an original variation of a historical design.

Another consideration when planning your quilting is the formality of the quilt. When we say "formal" and "informal" we are referring to the combination of elements that make up a quilt and give it either a highly organized, more structured appearance, or a loosely organized, more spontaneous appearance. We do not mean to attach any value judgment to either end of the formality scale. Some designs, such as freehand fans quilted without markings, seem most at home on informal scrap quilts. An informal cable, for instance, would just run off the edge at the corners instead of turning gracefully. A symmetrical medallion quilt with large plain areas is a more formal endeavor that seems to call for more elegant designs and formal corner resolutions.

You may or may not enjoy quilting. If you do not enjoy it much, or if you are making a "quick" quilt, you will probably seek the designs that give the strongest effect with the fewest stitches. If you enjoy quilting very much, you may seek designs for unexpected places, or double or triple normally single lines.

Sometimes we make a quilt specifically as a place to use a favorite quilting design, so we know before we even wash our yardage how the finished quilt will look. More often, however, we complete the piecing or appliqué before we start thinking about the quilting. Neither approach is the "correct" one for all quilts. It is not important how you work, only that you have a way of thinking about quilting designs, somewhere to start looking when you have no fixed ideas.

If you have an old quilt top you would like to quilt, one that you are sure would not be better unquilted, we recommend that you look at other quilts from the same period to see how they were quilted. One of our goals with this book is to help you design quilting patterns like those found on old quilts, so you will be able to come up with any design you might need. To help you do this we will cover the major design families of the tradition.

Some of our quilts in this book have fairly conventional quilting; some have unconventional quilting. In general we have tried to follow our own advice. That is, when we make a quilt in an old style, we try to make the quilting like that on the old quilts we are imitating. When we are creating a modern quilt that adheres to only its own rules, we let our imaginations run a little wilder.

COLUMNS, *(Plates 3-5)*, pages 14-15, for instance, is a modern adaptation of the "bars" design usually found only in the Old Order Amish tradition. Having changed the traditional design nearly beyond recognition, and having broad expanses of plain fabric in which to work, we decided to mix up new and old quilting designs in the same way. This design has an ordinary cable around the outside, and straight lines in the columns, meant to resemble classical architectural columns. The capitals, or top section, of the columns are made of mostly British quilting designs, such as spirals, paisleys, leaves, and odd feathered shapes.

After working your way through the exercises in the book and becoming familiar with both our techniques and our favorite patterns, you will easily be able to see the source material for the quilting designs in all our "arty," more original quilts, as well as for the more conventional ones.

Here is a brief review of the ideas you might consider when you are trying to decide how to quilt a top:

• The prominence of the quilting...will it be an important part of the finished quilt? Or will it be subsidiary to the patchwork?

• The style of the quilt...is it similar to an old or new quilt you have seen?

• The formality of the quilt...does it call for elegant, formal designs or freer, asymmetrical and informal ones?

• Do you enjoy quilting?

Answer these questions and you will be a long way toward choosing your quilting designs. We hope that once you have chosen them, this book will help you draft, mark, and quilt them.

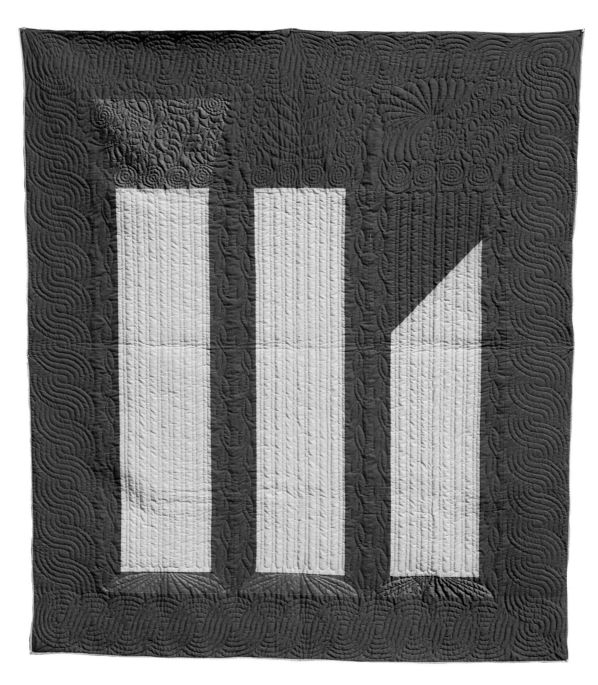

PLATE 4. Columns, 68" x 86". Made by the authors. Private Collection.
The idea for this quilt came during one of our discussions of quilt designs when one of us mentioned how "architectural" the Amish Bars pattern was. Changing the bars to columns was simple, and suggested the quilting designs. Classical cable and vine patterns surround the mock-Corinthian columns. The capitals of the columns are composed of freewheeling paisleys, flowers, feathers and leaves.
(Photo by the authors.)

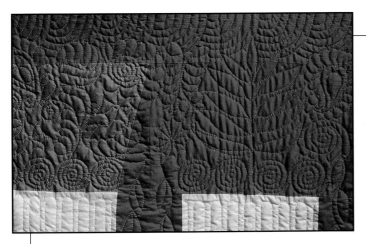

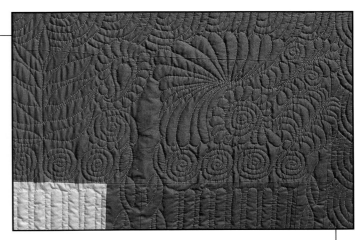

PLATE 5. Columns, detail.
(Photo by the authors.)

PLATE 6. Columns, detail.
(Photo by the authors.)

TOOLS YOU WILL NEED

You will need a few tools to perform the exercises in this book.

1. Paper. Many of the exercises can be done on typing paper. Some call for larger paper, and for that you can use a pad of newsprint such as art students use for drawing exercises. It should be at least 18" by 24". For our large drawings we use butcher paper that we buy in rolls from our local butcher. These rolls are 24" wide and about nine miles long. A roll costs about twenty-five dollars and is handy for many things. In fact, we use it to wrap presents at Christmas.

2. Tracing paper. Sometimes we ask you to trace something. For that you can use a small pad of tracing paper, the same size as typing paper.

3. Paper scissors. Remember that nothing dulls your fabric scissors like cutting paper. You will be doing a fair amount of paper cutting, so you will need a large pair of scissors dedicated to only that job.

4. Pencils and pens. Regular pencils work fine for most of our exercises. Sometimes you will need to darken lines so you can trace them onto the other side of a design. For that you can use a small felt-tip pen, the kind used for writing. Along with pencils you will also need an eraser.

5. Ruler. Our favorite rulers are made by the Omnigrid™ Company and are available at most quilt shops. They are clear and printed with accurate lines in black, outlined with yellow. We use these for all kinds of drafting and drawing on paper and fabric, as well as for guiding rotary cutters when we are making quilt tops. Nearly any kind of clear "quilter's" ruler will work, however.

6. Cardboard. We cut many shapes from cardboard. You can use cereal boxes, poster board, or any such single-thickness cardboard.

7. Compass. Compasses come in a wide variety of styles and qualities. If you use an inexpensive one like the ones most of us used in school, it will probably have an arc of metal with measurements on it. These, we have found, are notoriously unreliable. Whatever type you use, always open it to the directed distance and place it against a ruler so you can see exactly how far apart the points really are.

CHAPTER 2

STRAIGHT-LINE DESIGNS

PLATE 7. Pinwheel Star, detail. Full quilt shown on page 24.

Many quilts, old and new, are quilted with simple (and sometimes not so simple) straight lines. The lines may be parallel, they may cross at various angles, they may meander a bit. Straight lines have probably been used so much throughout history because quilting is, among other things, functional – that is, one of its jobs is to join three layers of fabric together, and it is not necessary to use fancy designs in the process. Many quilters of the past chose not to explore new ways of quilting, but instead used a simple straight-line design over and over on quilt after quilt.

Quilting's practical use, before the introduction of modern battings, was twofold: first, it held the three layers – top, batting, and backing – together, and second, it kept the batting from shifting and bunching, by enclosing it in small pockets or narrow channels. On the earliest known quilt, made around 0 B.C. in Scythia, the border is crosshatched. A likeness of an even earlier example, an Egyptian ivory carving of a mummy, has a figure wrapped in what appears to be a quilted cloth. It, too, is crosshatched. Crosshatching and other straight line variations are common today as well, especially among quilt artists, for whom the straight-quilting line is much more palatable than the feather wreath, or hearts.

Even when other designs are used, straight lines have often been used as "filler" behind them. Or, a border might have an elaborate design while the interior is quilted with crosshatching. In short, straight-line designs have many uses. They are the platform upon which many other designs stand.

In our scheme of categorizing quilting designs, we include outline quilting, stitching in the ditch and criss-cross lines in the straight-line family. All three designs have been in use as long as patchwork quilts have been made on this continent. They have several advantages over more complicated designs: they are in keeping with many styles, they are easily quilted in hoops or frames, and they do not have to be marked on the quilt top.

OUTLINE QUILTING

The design of choice for many quilters, outline quilting is merely quilting around the inside of each patch for piecework, or around the outside of each patch for appliqué. This has also been called "self quilting." If your quilt top is heavily pieced, you may want to outline quilt to avoid quilting through seams. DIAMOND FOUR PATCH, a simple variation of the classic four patch, is outline quilted *(Plate 8)*. Notice that the outline is far enough from the seam to miss the seam allowance, which means that its quilter never had to quilt through more than the three layers of top, batting, and back. Quilting across a seam can mean pushing the needle through four, five or more layers of fabric where the seam allowances meet. Also, the quilter of our DIAMOND FOUR PATCH let the quilting design itself; that is, she used the same design in the alternate blocks that the outline quilting created in the pieced blocks.

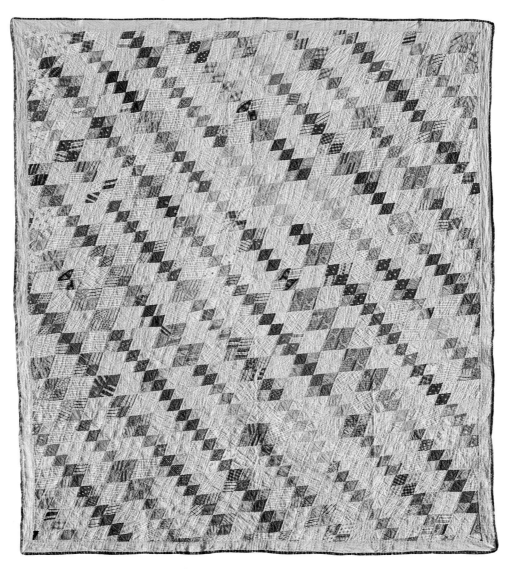

PLATE 8. Diamond Four Patch, 74" x 87", c.1875-1900.
This quilt exemplifies the attitude toward quiltmaking we find most stimulating: the quiltmaker had to figure out some way to resolve the sides, so she just made extra and cut them off straight. What is interesting, aside from the quilt itself, is the fact of its originality. The quilting is simple, functional outline quilting. The design is the same in the pieced and the plain blocks.

Outline quilting is sometimes all you need, especially with a quilt like ROLLING STAR (*Plate 9*). For larger patches, double outlines or even triple outlines can fill in the space easily, as you can see on the border of our TULIP SAMPLER quilt (*Plate 48, p. 121*). Any pieced shape can be outline quilted. Grandmother's Flower Garden quilts were nearly all quilted with outlines around each hexagon. If a block has some very small pieces, you might want to outline some and leave others unquilted, or just outline one edge of the small pieces.

Appliqué makes an obvious candidate for outline quilting. This approach is usually supplemented with some kind of background quilting, such as cross-

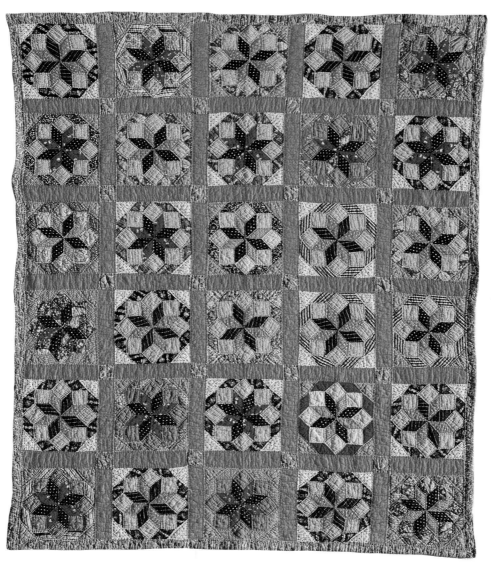

PLATE 9. Rolling Star, 74" x 86", c. 1940. Maker unknown.
Every patch in this quilt is outlined. The lattice has a few additional quilting lines, which form a sort of ladder. With such a graphically strong and intricate quilt top, simple, functional quilting is all that is necessary.

hatching or simple diagonal lines (*Plate 11*). These outlines, too, are sometimes doubled. And the outlines are not always on the outside of appliquéd patches. Our foremothers and forefathers in quilting were not as dedicated to the proposition that one should avoid seams as quilters are today. Many appliqués are outlined both inside and out, sometimes with double lines on both sides, but usually with single lines (*Plate 10*).

Some quilters prefer to mark every line they are going to quilt. Thus, tools

PLATE 10. Tulip Pot, detail.

PLATE 11. Tulip Pot, 83" x 88", c.1875. Maker unknown.
Though the batting in this quilt is quite heavy, the maker decided to quilt very close lines all over, about ³⁄₁₆". The quilting does not go over the appliqué. Instead, the appliqué is outlined inside and outside of each patch.

have been devised to make it easy to mark these quarter-inch lines. There are many see-through rulers, ¼" plexiglass rods, and even ¼" masking tape that you can press on along a seam and quilt beside. We used to mark outlines, but discovered that it was not necessary. After all, you have a guideline ¼" away! We find that our outlines vary only slightly from patch to patch, so slightly that the difference is difficult to measure. Even a long outline, such as that around the body of a quilt on a plain border, can be easily "eyeballed."

Freehand quilting these lines not only speeds up and simplifies quiltmaking, but it also eliminates marked lines on the quilt top, (if you mark them) or the possibility of getting tape residue on the fabric (if you use the masking tape method). If you take the tape off as soon as you are done quilting and at the end of every

PLATE 12. Trip Around the World, 72" x 82", top c.1935. Maker unknown; quilted by the authors.
One of the most common quilt patterns of the depression era, Trip Around the World was almost always quilted with simple criss-crossing lines. We decided to treat it the way we thought the original quilter would have.

quilting session, this should not happen. But we have known quilters who left the tape in place for a month, perhaps in the sun at some point, and found a sticky residue on the fabric when they peeled it off. We find it best to avoid problems like this by freehand quilting everything we can.

STITCHING IN THE DITCH

"Stitching in the ditch" is, as far as we know, a fairly recent term for the practice of quilting along the seam between two patches. The idea is to quilt on the side away from the direction in which the seam allowances have been pressed. If you quilt close enough to the seam, your stitches will be hidden by the puffy seam on the unquilted side. Some quilters prefer stitching in the ditch because they are self-conscious about their stitches and they want them hidden as much as possible. Also, some quilters just do not want the quilting to interfere with the pieced design.

Sometimes the ditch may be a logical place for a quilting line. Sooner or later, though, most quilters find themselves needing to quilt a design on a plain border or in a plain block where there are no ditches in which to quilt. So we think it is best to have other options available when you consider how to quilt any quilt.

CRISS-CROSS

Many pieced designs contain squares. These can be outlined, but another common way to quilt them is to criss-cross, or put an "x" through them *(Plate 12)*. Like outline quilting, these lines are usually marked, but we have found that we can criss-cross all but the largest squares with no marking at all. Most pieced squares are no larger than 2" or 3" on a side, and, for us, the diagonal of one of these is a short enough distance that we don't wander too far from our intended line.

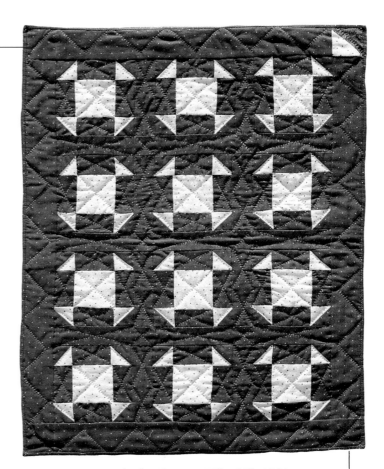

PLATE 13. Puss in the Corner, 17" x 22", 1988. Made by Gwen Marston.

Squares that seem too large for criss-crossing can be outlined and criss-crossed. Rectangles are often criss-crossed as well, with an elongated "x" that can be very pleasing in an overall design *(Plate 13)*. If you have always marked these lines, it can be intimidating to consider quilting them freehand. You might want to try it first on a small quilt; you will find that it only takes a few squares to become comfortable with the notion.

FREEHAND

Actually, all types of straight-line designs can be quilted freehand. We often quilt large triangles with echo lines about ½" apart. We used to mark these, but have since found that there is no need to. With larger designs, you just have to realize that the effect of freehand quilting and marked quilting is different. The freehand lines on the old STAR quilt shown below are perfectly compatible with its free, loose piecing (Plate 14). Note the chopped triangle corners, the nipped points of the stars. Once you get away from the idea that there are right and wrong ways to make quilts, you can appreciate this kind of quilt because of the way it is made, not in spite of it.

Freehand lines do not need to look haphazard or messy. Sometimes they impart just the right energetic element a bold quilt needs. (Plates 15, 16)

PLATE 14. Star, 78" x 92", c.1880. Maker unknown.
Everything about this quilt suggests that it was made to be used. The piecing is fairly slapdash, the batting is heavy, and the quilting is simple, freehand straight lines. With all that, it remains one of our favorites, because of its graphic strength.

PLATE 15. Rose, 76" x 80", c.1875,
Signed "E. L.". Maker unknown.

As on many old appliqués, the quilting on this goes right across the appliquéd patches. Notice, for instance, the feather wreaths that are quilted over the small corner plumes. The quilting is mostly on a "feather" theme, from small, scattered pinwheels to large feathered plumes over the center block.

PLATE 16. Rose, back, detail.

The quilting is only marginally related to the appliqué design. In general, where there is appliqué there is fancy quilting, but the quilting is laid across the appliqué and ignores its design.

PLATE 17. Pinwheel Star, 70" x 80", 1988.
Made by the authors.
The quilting designs here are all made of simple straight lines. The block pieces are criss-crossed and/or outlined. The borders have triple diagonals. Sometimes simple is strongest.

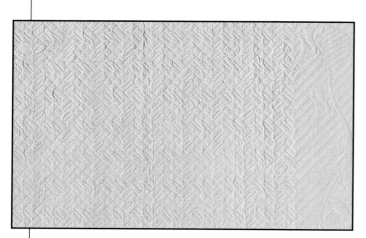

PLATE 18. Pinwheel Star, back, detail.
The criss-cross and outline quilting of the patches in the top form a pleasing design on the back.

Most often we mark our straight lines, but only those that need to be marked. PINWHEEL STAR, which has triple diagonals on the border, needed to have only the center line of each set of three marked. *(Plate 16)* We could then quilt lines freehand on each side of the marked diagonals. All the outline quilting and criss-crossing in the blocks were done freehand.

Quilters long ago discovered that it was easier to quilt on the bias than on the straight. That is why so many quilts have diagonal line quilting rather than perpendicular. Quilting on the straight of the goods may be harder because there is no "give" for the needle when one tries to force it up and down through the layers. We do not know for sure. What we *do* know is that lines quilted on the straight of the goods are more difficult to quilt, that the stitches are usually slightly longer than others and that they actually look different than stitches on the bias.

For those reasons diagonal quilting lines are much more often used than perpendicular ones. Borders, for instance, are usually quilted with diagonals instead of perpendiculars. Crosshatching is usually done on the diagonal instead of the straight.

It would seem that nothing could be easier than to mark straight lines on a quilt top. But if you have ever tried it you know how quickly you can lose the angle with which you started. Because of small, accumulated errors, the lines can quickly begin leaning out of control.

We use a simple tool made of cardboard to keep our straight lines parallel and at the proper angle. We call it an "angle keeper."

You can make your own:

1. Make a 45-degree angle by folding a piece of paper as shown *(Figure 1)*.

2. Transfer the angle to a piece of cardboard *(Figure 2)*.

3. Using a see-through ruler, draw a parallel line beside the angle, as far away as you want the diagonals to be separated. For instance, if you want them ¾" apart, then make this line ¾" from the angle *(Figure 3)*.

4. Draw another line the same distance above the base line *(Figure 4)*.

5. Cut out the shape *(Figure 5)*.

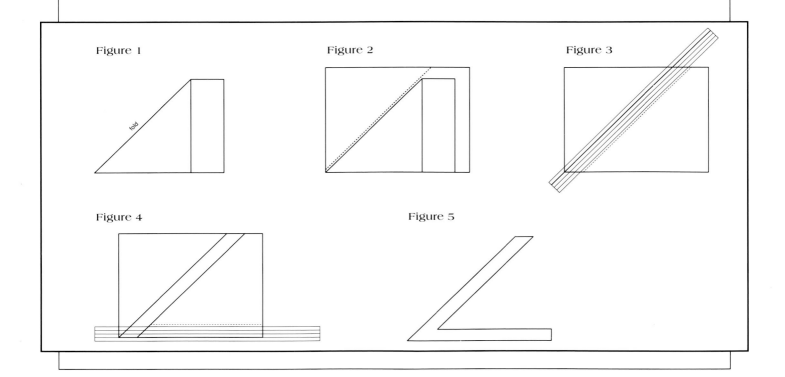

Figure 1

Figure 2

Figure 3

Figure 4

Figure 5

The angle keeper will keep all your diagonals aligned. Some plastic quilter's rulers have lines marked on them for the same purpose, but we find it is even more accurate to have the cardboard edge to line up with the border or block *(Plate 17)*.

Try using the angle keeper to mark a series of diagonal lines on a long piece of paper *(Figures 6,7)*. Notice how if one of your lines goes astray, you can see and correct it immediately.

The family of diagonal variations is very large, but there are a few patterns that have been used over and over. Crosshatching, hanging diamonds, double diagonals, plaids – all are easily marked with the angle keeper and can be used on blocks and borders, as fillers behind other quilting designs, or as all-over patterns. You can practice these on newsprint.

CROSSHATCHING

Crosshatching is made by marking diagonal or perpendicular lines first in one direction, then the other *(Figure 8)*. Simply flip your angle keeper to make the second group of lines. If you start the second group at the base of one of the

PLATE 19.
The angle keeper in action.

lines from the first group, the lines will form perfect squares, on point, along the edge of the design.

HANGING DIAMONDS

To mark hanging diamonds you will need a straight angle keeper. That is, you will need an angle keeper that will let you mark right angles. It should look like this *(Figure 9)*, and it should be the same width as the other angle keeper.

Mark a series of diagonals as in Figure 7. Then start in the same place with the straight angle keeper and mark a series of straight lines. You will see that the second straight line starts before the second diagonal. That is how this pattern works. Continue marking straight lines and you will see how the diamonds that are formed seem to fall row by row against the edge *(Figure 10)*.

DOUBLE DIAGONALS

Diagonal lines are often doubled or tripled. There are a couple of approaches you can take if you want to double yours.

First, you can just mark a series of diagonals as above, then quilt the double lines freehand. This is easier to do than you might think. Make sure to double each line on the same side as the one before. If you try this you will see that quilting is a slow enough process that you cannot wander too far from where you intend to be.

Second, you can mark every line. To do this, mark the first line, then move the angle keeper a little bit to the right and mark the double line *(Figure 11)*, as well as the second main line. Repeat. In other words, once you have the first line drawn, just scoot the angle keeper a little to the right and mark on both sides of it. If you want to be absolutely accurate with your measurements, use a see-through ruler to position the angle keeper just less than ¼" from the original line. To us, a full

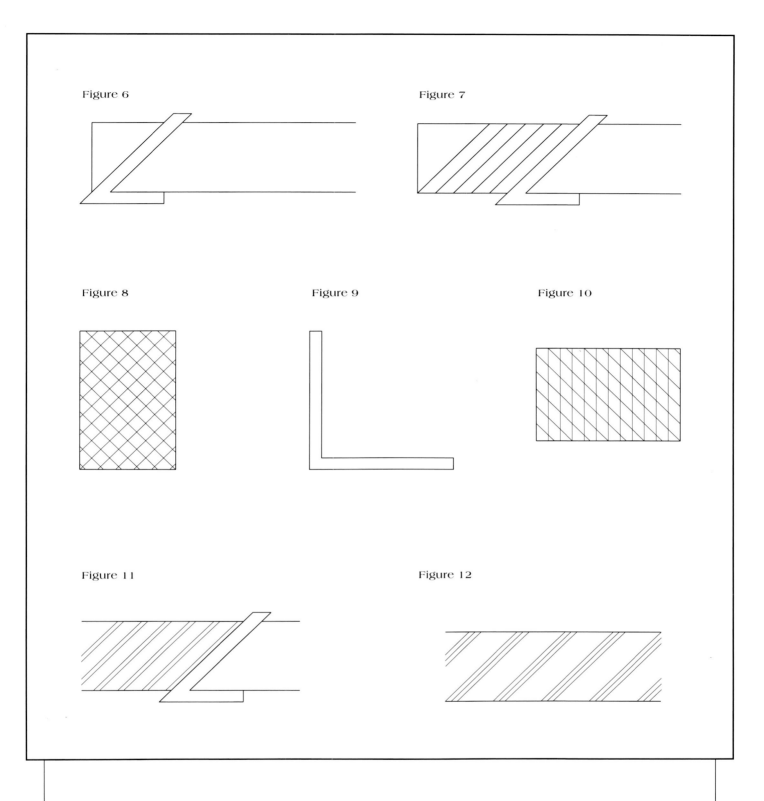

Figure 6

Figure 7

Figure 8

Figure 9

Figure 10

Figure 11

Figure 12

¼" seems too wide, and ⅛" seems too narrow. See what you think.

Triple diagonals can also be quilted freehand once you have the initial lines in place. Just quilt new lines on each side of the original (*Figure 12*). Or you can mark the lines as with double diagonals. Once

again, you can "eyeball" the spacing or you can measure it. In general, triple diagonals need a fairly wide angle keeper, 1¼" to 1½", to allow for the extra lines.

We have seen quilts with as many as five very close diagonals, then a space, then five more "quintuple diagonals."

SIMPLE PLAID

This design could also be called "double crosshatching." With it, you must mark all the lines as you go. Mark double diagonals in one direction *(Figure 13)* and then the other *(Figure 14)*.

Simple plaid is one of the most effective of all filling patterns. It takes twice as long to quilt as single crosshatching, but the effect is incomparably rich.

BROKEN PLAID

Broken plaid is little-used on either antique or contemporary quilts. Perhaps for that reason, it is one of our favorites. It is made by doubling every other line, in both directions. You must mark the doublings as you go, not after you have the original diagonals in place.

Start with a single line, then another. Now double the second line *(Figure 15)*. Do this again. Mark a section as shown. Flip your angle keeper over and repeat, doubling every other line as you go *(Figure 16)*.

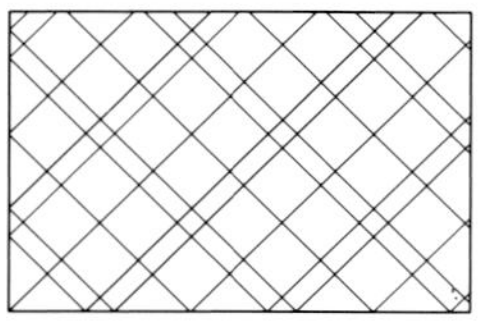

Keep in mind that all single-line patterns can be doubled or tripled. We have seen triple hanging diamonds, for example, and we have quilted a triple plaid design.

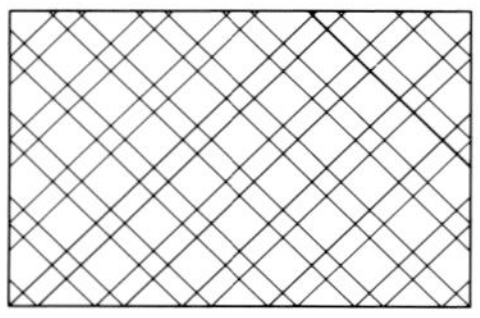

As we said earlier, all these patterns can be used for entire quilts or for any part of a quilt. They can be used alone or with other quilting designs. There are different characteristics, however, within all-over designs, border designs, and block fillers that are not so universal. We will treat those as separate categories.

ALL-OVER PATTERNS

In the past, a common way to mark any long, straight lines was to "snap" them with a chalk line. With the quilt top in a frame, a chalk-dusted string could be held taut from corner to corner and snapped to make a line. Joe's mother remembers her mother snapping quilts with a string dusted with flour. One problem with snapping is that it is difficult to keep the successive lines accurately aligned. The solution is to use an angle keeper instead.

For lines that cover an entire quilt top you will need a bit of equipment: an angle keeper, a *reverse* angle keeper, and a long, straight board, about 1" x 2" x 8'. The reverse angle keeper is the opposite side of the cardboard you cut out for the original angle keeper. Follow the same procedure as before, but measure and cut the open angle, not the closed one *(Figure 17)*. The "one by two" mentioned above should only cost a couple of dollars at a lumberyard, and is vital to marking long lines. This is the same kind of board used to make a quilting frame, so we just use a quilting board for the job.

We have also found that it is vastly easier and quicker to mark long lines with two people than with only one. Any friend or family member will do – the person

Figure 13

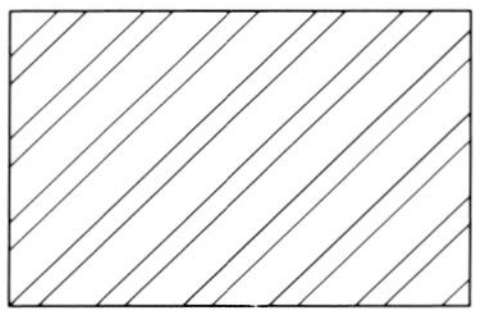

Figure 14

Figure 15

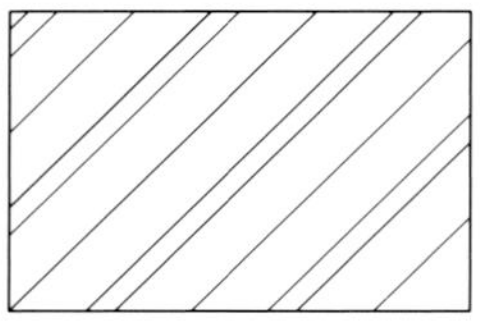

Figure 16

need not be interested in quilts, just willing to help hold and move one end of the board. Each person should have a regular and a reverse angle keeper.

We like to mark long lines on the floor where we have lots of room to lay the top out flat and work all the way around it. We will use crosshatching for a basic example of all-over marking.

If your quilt top, like most, is rectangular, it is helpful to measure a square from which to start. Measure the exact width, then make a small mark that distance up the long sides. This gives you a point from which to start.

Lay the board in a lower corner, diagonally to the mark on the opposite side. Draw the line beside it *(Figure 18)*. Now you should be able to use your angle keepers as shown in *Figure 19* to move the board to the next position. Remove the angle keepers and mark the next line. Continue in this way in both directions from the first line until you have covered the entire top. Repeat the process, starting from the other corner and the mark on the other side *(Figure 20)*.

Sometimes you will need the regular angle keeper, sometimes the reverse. Try it and you will see.

All the patterns discussed can be marked in this fashion. It is almost essential to have two people working on this type of project. Moving the board into place each time is very difficult alone.

Because it is easiest to make the first lines from corner to corner, much crosshatching has been done with diamonds instead of squares *(Figure 21)*. You can make custom angle keepers for this job by laying the board carefully in position, slipping a piece of cardboard under it in one corner and tracing the angle you need. Mark lines in both directions to form diamonds.

Another way to mark diagonals over an entire quilt top is to start with a

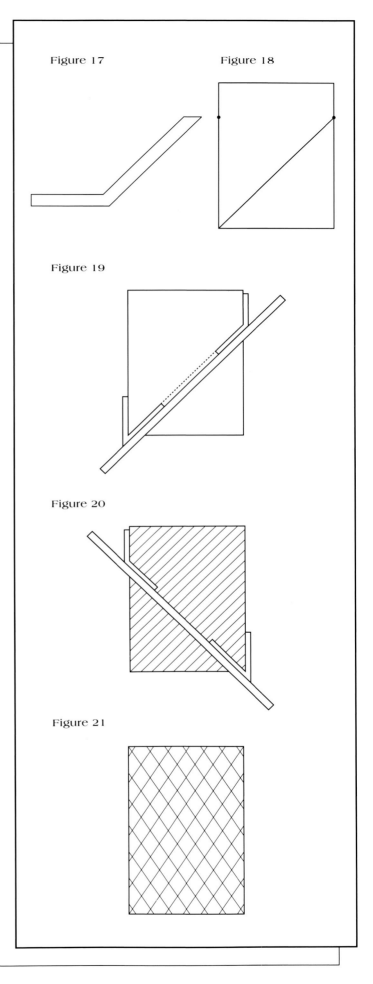

Figure 17   Figure 18

Figure 19

Figure 20

Figure 21

Figure 22

Figure 23

Figure 24

Figure 25

However, this time start with four lines going midpoint to midpoint on the sides (*Figure 24*). Now you can fill in with parallel lines, inward and outward from the originals (*Figure 25*).

BORDERS

Like all-over patterns, borders can also be quilted with crosshatching, plaids, hanging diamonds, etc. Unsurprisingly, the simplest design – single diagonals – has long been the most popular for borders. We take one of two basic approaches when we mark diagonals on our quilts: old-fashioned or modern.

In the last century, when quilters were much less concerned with symmetry than they are today, diagonals were often quilted freehand in one direction around the border (*Figure 26*). To mark these, just start in one corner with your angle keeper and work your way all the way around the quilt.

Another old-fashioned pattern was the result of quilting in a frame. Quilters

corner-to-corner "X" as shown in *Figure 22* and fill in the spaces with "tents" (*Figure 23*). You may find it helpful to mark light lines across the middle of the quilt top, so you can see where to change directions.

Start with the same light middle lines to make our final all-over variation.

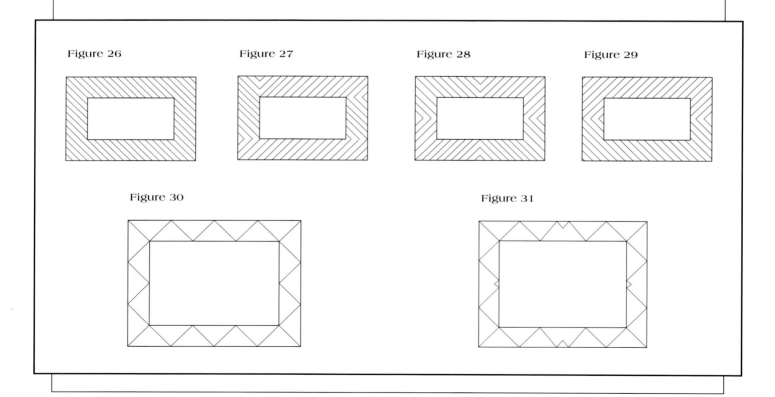

Figure 26

Figure 27

Figure 28

Figure 29

Figure 30

Figure 31

would start in one corner and quilt diagonals clear down to the other corner. Then they would slip around the corner and quilt to the next one. If you work this way all around the quilt you will create a design something like that shown in *Figure 27*.

Modern quilters seem to prefer a more symmetrical approach. One common technique is to change directions in the middle of each border. If you start in the corners and mark towards the middles, all four corners and middles will be the same. We usually put a pin at the mid-point so we can tell when to stop. The lines will meet and form perfect "tents" in the middle of each border *(Figure 28)*.

If your quilt has a definite top and bottom, you could try changing directions on the top and bottom only, as shown in *Figure 29*. This time you start with the angle keeper in the lower two corners and work to the middle of the top, then to the middle of the bottom. You may want to mark the midpoints where you want to change directions with a light line instead of a pin.

Use your angle keeper imaginatively and you will come up with many variations. We like to flip-flop it to make a zigzag line on the border, once again starting in the corners and working to the middles *(Figure 30)*. Many quilts will not work out so symmetrically. For these, let the lines just collide in the middle *(Figure 31)*. We will talk about the mid section in a moment. The triangles can be filled with the design of your choice, but, since we are using the angle keeper, let's start with it.

First, use the angle keeper to fill in each triangle with opposing parallel lines *(Figure 32)*. This is a pleasant design that works on many kinds of quilts.

Second, flip-flop the angle keeper within each triangle to make "tents" *(Figure 33)*. This works best for fairly wide borders.

Third, mark one line as shown in *Figure 34*, then flip the angle keeper and mark another, crossing the first line *(Figure 35)*. Flip again and do not cross the previous line *(Figure 36)*. Continue doing this until the triangle is filled *(Figure 37)*. This is a beautiful design, useful for formal, elegant quilts.

The midpoint of your border will probably look something like *Figure 38*,

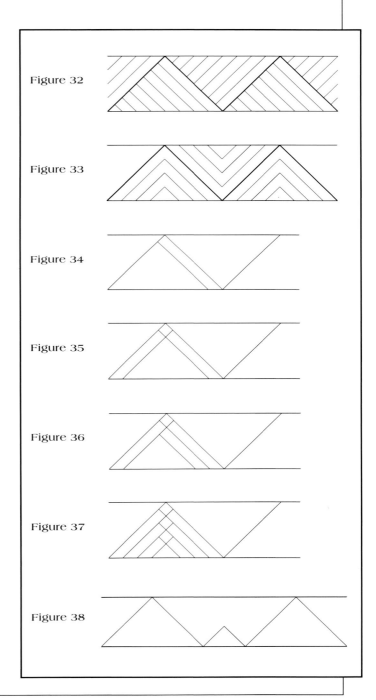

Figure 32

Figure 33

Figure 34

Figure 35

Figure 36

Figure 37

Figure 38

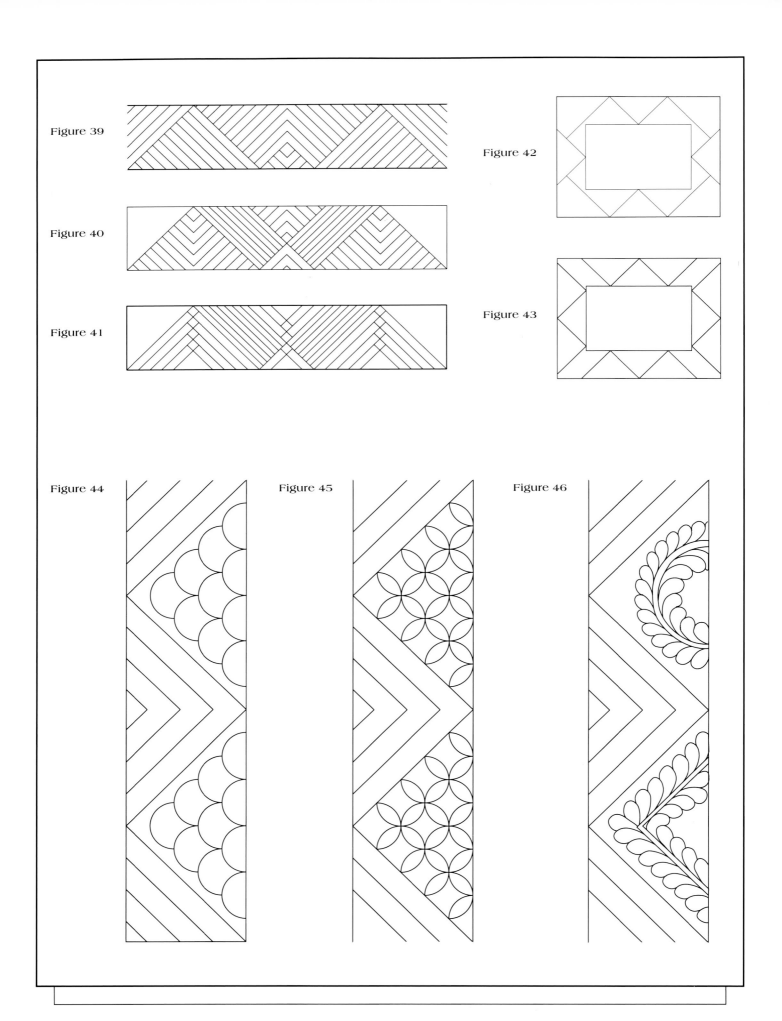

Figure 39

Figure 40

Figure 41

Figure 42

Figure 43

Figure 44

Figure 45

Figure 46

so it is time to invent a "middle resolution." One simple way to do this is to fool around with the design you used up to that point, as shown in *Figures 39, 40, 41*.

There are no simple formulas for middle resolutions. You just need to experiment with elements of your design to see how they can be shortened or lengthened, stretched or compressed. With straight lines like this it is not too difficult to come up with solutions to the problem. Try taking one of these ideas and applying it to your design, adding or subtracting lines as required.

Another way to approach the problem of making symmetrical borders is to start in the middle and work outward toward the ends. In this case you will need to invent a corner resolution if your design does not land squarely in the corner *(Figure 42)*. With this approach you get another chance to make an adjustment: you can try starting in the middle of a triangle *(Figure 43)*. No matter what happens in the corners, straight-line variations are nearly always appropriate and functional for filling in odd spaces.

These triangles are the quilting equivalent of pie shells; they can be filled with whatever you like. Reaching into upcoming chapters, we could fill every other one with clamshells *(Figure 44)*, teacups *(Figure 45)*, or feathers *(Figure 46)*. Keep this in mind as we explore other designs. We mixed up several fillers on the border of our SNOWBALL quilt *(Plate 20, page 34)*.

BLOCK FILLERS

Like the other parts of a quilt, blocks can be filled with any of the standard straight-line variations we showed earlier: crosshatching, hanging diamonds, plaids, double or triple diagonals, etc.

Blocks can also be treated as miniatures of all-over patterns. That is, you can make an "X" and fill the four spaces with "tents" *(Figure 47)*. Or you can start with lines from midpoint to midpoint on the sides *(Figure 48)*. We have used this design on a number of appliqué quilts that were set block-to-block. The quilting then tends to camouflage the piecing seam *(Plate 21, page 34)*.

Figure 47

Figure 48

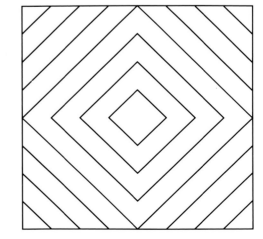

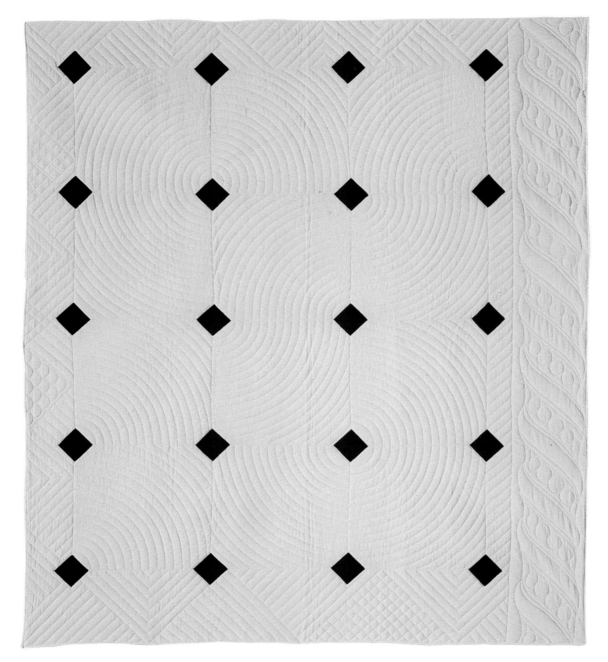

PLATE 20. Snowball, 67" x 75", 1986. Made by the authors.
For a show where we made modern versions of classic quilts, we made this original interpretation of the Snowball pattern. The design, of course, was taken from a tile pattern. (We sometimes call this "The Bathroom Floor Quilt.") With virtually all the action in this quilt taking place in the quilting, we used a few of our favorite patterns. A fan variation swirls around the middle of the quilt, and three sides have diagonal variations. The fourth has a representation of an architectural column.

PLATE 21. Rose Wreath, 78" x 78", 1990. Made by Mary Schafer;
quilted by Elizabeth Miller.

Mary Schafer recreated an old Rose Wreath in her collection – shown in *American Beauties: Rose and Tulip Quilts*, p. 27 – and marked the quilting much like the original. Notice the curved fill lines around the feathered vine border, This diagonal line treatment of the blocks obscures the seams between the blocks, giving instead the impression of a continuous field upon which the appliqué rests.

Figure 49

We have limited this section to straight lines only, but in practice few quilts are quilted with only one type of design. Straight lines are usually used as the "frame" upon which the more elaborate quilting designs are built. We cannot repeat often enough how important it is to look at the quilting designs on old and new quilts to see how other quilters have used the kind of design you are considering. We always find new ways to use quilting designs by looking in our books, even when studying quilts we have seen a hundred times.

You can start the same way – midpoint to midpoint – and fill in the corners with lines, but leave the center to be filled with another design (*Figure 49*).

The angle keeper is extremely helpful when you need to invent block fillers. Work with paper the size of your block. A few possibilities are shown in *Figure 50*, on page 37.

The patches that make up pieced blocks can be outlined, wholly or partially, or criss-crossed, or worked with a combination of the two. This is often effective, but you may want to try some other treatments. Before outline quilting became so nearly universal, quilters often quilted single or double lines across pieced blocks (*Figure 51*). Midwest Amish quilters, until 1940 or so, quilted nearly all their pieced blocks this way.

Some blocks are filled with diamonds. Diamonds result when you make an angle keeper with any angle other than a 45° angle. The diamonds in *Figure 52* were made with a 60° angle keeper, which we derived by using the 60° angle on an Omnigrid™ ruler, but any angle will work. You can use diamonds like this on borders as well.

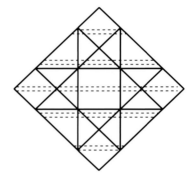

Figure 51

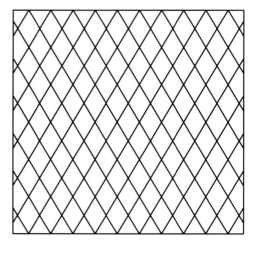

Figure 52

Figure 50

CHAPTER 3

CIRCLE DESIGNS

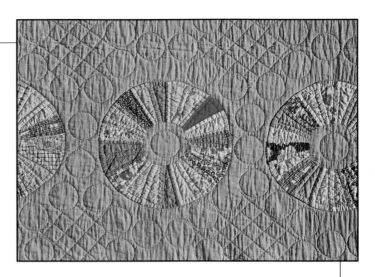

PLATE 22. Dresden Plate, detail, 66" x 84", c.1935. Made by Minnie Roe.

Another family of quilting designs is based on the circle, or parts of a circle. Some of these designs, like teacup, fan or clamshell, have been used by artisans for many thousands of years, and have been adopted by quiltmakers and given new names. Few of these can easily be quilted freehand.

Circles have been used in primarily two ways: either they float freely in spaces that need filler, or they overlap to form a "chain mail" type of design. PRINCESS FEATHER (Plate 23), made in the mid-1800's, has circles about the size of the end of a thread spool. We think the quilter probably marked these as she quilted, by scratching with her needle around her spool of quilting thread. Needle marks do not last very long, but they would be fine for small circles like this.

The woman who quilted the DRESDEN PLATE (Plate 22), in the late 1930's used something larger for her circles, perhaps a juice glass. There are faint traces of pencil lines, which show

that she probably marked the circles before she put the quilt in the frame.

We have seen overlapped circles used to fill narrow borders on Amish quilts (Figure 53). Small circles, about the size of the end of a thimble, have been used to fill spaces or even for all-over quilting. Circles are rarely designed to work out evenly at the sides of old quilts. They simply start and stop with partial circles wherever they happen to fall.

Gwen's Mennonite quilting teachers used cups, saucers and plates to mark various circles on quilt tops. This is part of a long quilting tradition of "making do" with anything handy. We have been known to use plates and platters ourselves. For small circles, though, we prefer a plastic template sheet we found in a drafting supply store. It has circles from 1" to 3½" in diameter. It is transparent, so we can see to align it where we want before marking the circle with a pencil. We also use homemade cardboard circles, as discussed in the next section, and shown in Plate 24.

PLATE 23. Princess Feather, 80" x 82", c.1875-1900. Maker unknown.
This exuberant appliqué quilt has many quilting designs that contribute to its energetic, playful character. The plumes have a double zig-zag spine. The borders have small circles, possibly marked with a thread spool. The criss-cross background quilting forms squares ranging from ⅜" to ½". Most of the appliqué is outlined both inside and outside the shapes. Our favorite design here is small feather wreath, double quilted on the outside and filled with a tripled circle.

Figure 53

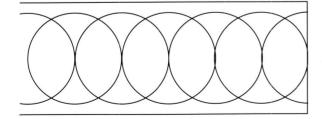

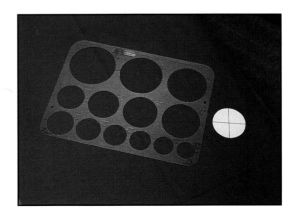

PLATE 24. Circle templates.

Figure 54

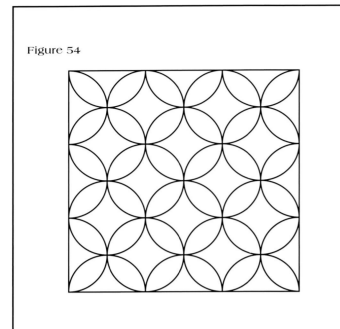

Figure 55

Figure 56

Figure 57

Figure 58

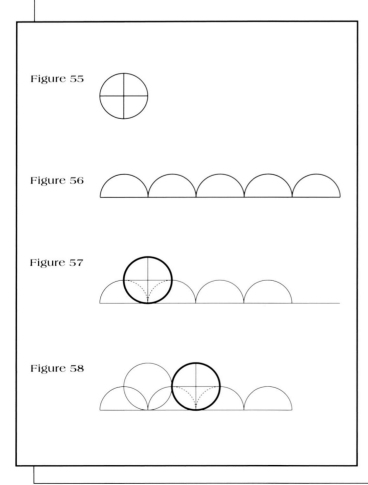

TEACUP

One circle design is often called "Teacup" here in the United States, but in England it is called "Wine Glass" *(Figure 54)*. The pleasing effect of interlocking circles has made this pattern a favorite with quilters of all kinds, down to the present time.

You could use a teacup or wine glass to mark this on your quilt top, but it would be difficult going. We find that it is easier to mark circles with a template. We make ours out of cardboard and draw "crosshairs" on them. We make a number of sizes, but a 2" circle will work for the next exercise *(Figure 55)*. With this, we can either mark directly on the quilt top, or on paper to make a pattern to transfer to the quilt top. Of course we prefer marking directly on the top whenever we can, but it is easiest to practice on paper.

Start by marking a row of half circles along the bottom edge of your paper *(Figure 56)*. The crosshairs make it simple to line up the template each time. Now, start with full circles lined up as shown *(Figure 57)*. You will have three points to check: the valley between half circles, and the tops of the two half circles. Draw around the template, then move to the next position and draw the next circle *(Figure 58)*. If you find yourself getting a bit out of alignment, just force the next circle closer to where it should be. Continue to make rows of circles until you have filled your space.

As with most quilting designs, Teacup can be made formal or informal by controlling its symmetry. On NEW CROSS AND CROWN, *(Plate 25, page 42)*, the quilter made her template a size that would divide evenly into the space to be filled, enabling the circles to meet the edges of the square. If you have a 12" block, for instance, you could use 1", 2", 3", 4", or 6" circles to fill it evenly. On

DANAE (*Plate 26,* page 43), we used a circle that did *not* divide evenly into the space, which left us with partial circles at one edge (*Figure 59*). Either way is fine; you need only to decide what kind of effect you want.

Teacup is often used to fill the triangular space around the feather in the middle of an Amish Center Diamond (*Figure 60*). Plain blocks on all kinds of quilts are also commonly filled with it. Teacup is sometimes, but not often, found on borders.

All circular patterns in this chapter can be frustrating to quilters who want every part of their quilt to "work out." That is because these designs are based on circles, while most quilts are based on rectangles. If you are marking a teacup all over a quilt, there will come a point where you have a partial circle (see *Figure 59*). That is simply what happens when you are working with circular designs in quilts; the designs are round, quilts are square.

Figure 59

Figure 60

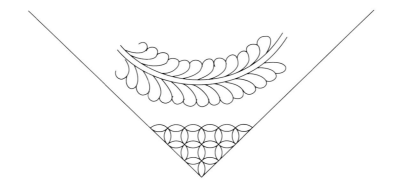

PLATE 25. New Cross and Crown, 68" x 73", c.1875-1900. Maker unknown.
The maker of this quilt worked the quilting designs carefully to be symmetrical and to fit the quilt. The cable on the outer border, unlike many of the period, turns its corners smoothly. The teacup quilting fits the plain blocks exactly. And the diagonal variation in the pieced blocks is clever and neat. For similar ideas, see Figure 50. The blocks are simple nine patches with appliquéd triangles added to make the pattern.

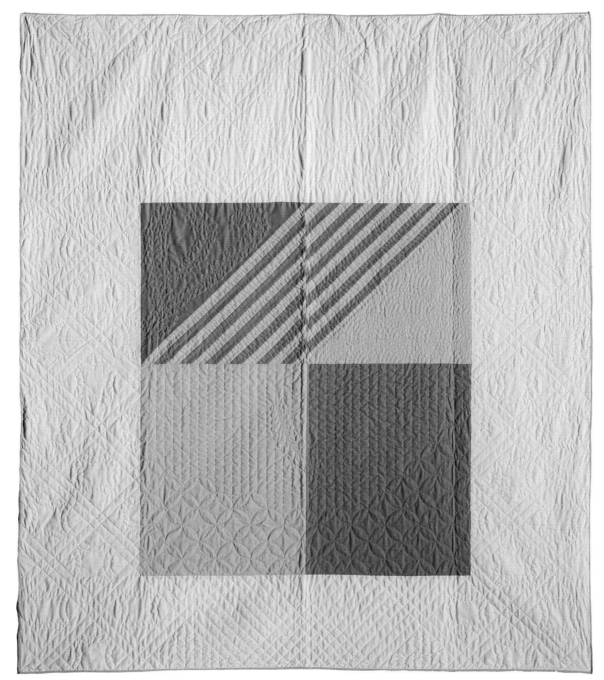

PLATE 26. Danae, 69" x 82", 1985. Made by the authors.
One of a series of quilts about Zeus's affairs with mortal women, this quilt is an abstract look into the underground brass chamber in which Danae was imprisoned by her father. Zeus turned himself into a "shower of gold" and rained in through the air vents. Later, Danae gave birth to Perseus. Our idea was to use traditional quilting designs in an unconventional way. Notice the teacup, fans, and feathered tendrils in the colored section.

Figure 61

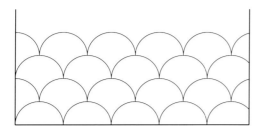

Figure 62

Figure 63

Figure 64

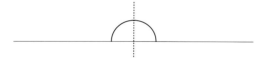

Figure 65

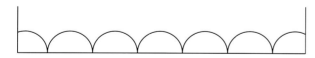

Figure 66

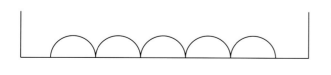

CLAMSHELL

We see clamshell *(Figure 61)*, also called "shell," even more often than teacup. You can use the same circle template with crosshairs to mark it. Start as before with a row of half circles along the bottom edge of your paper. Align the template as before with the three points as shown *(Figure 62)*. This time, however, trace only around the top half of the circle *(Figure 63)*.

We have used quite small circles for clamshell templates – nickels, and even dimes. On small-scale quilts, small clamshells look great. The clamshell quilting on our STAR AND CHERRIES quilt *(Sets and Borders*, p. 49) has clamshells marked with both nickels and dimes.

Clamshell and teacup usually fill an entire area. If you want both sides of the space to be the same you can start in the middle *(Figure 64)*. You can either run the design right to the edge, as in *Figure 65*, or stop with the last full unit *(Figure 66)*. Clamshells form a triangle naturally if you build rows with one fewer each time. For a symmetrical square you can use four of

Figure 67

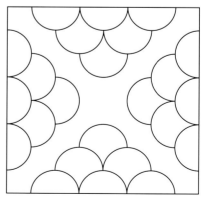

these triangles *(Figure 67)*.

A great way to use clamshells is to place a single row of them around anything: borders *(Figure 68)*, blocks *(Figure 69)*, triangles *(Figure 70)*, lattice *(Figure 71)*, or anywhere you like. One of Mary Schafer's techniques is to put a line of clamshells around the inside of an outer border, then send her diagonal fill lines out from it *(Figure 72)*.

Clamshells are sometimes doubled *(Figure 73)*. Just mark one set of shells and quilt the doubling lines freehand, keeping the second line about ⅛" inside the first.

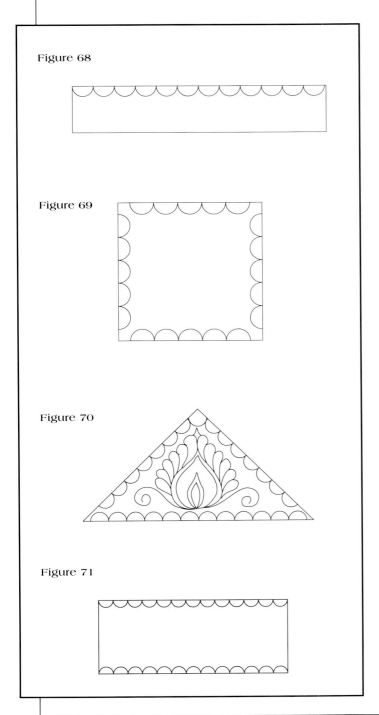

Figure 68

Figure 69

Figure 70

Figure 71

Figure 72

Figure 73

CHAPTER 4

FAN DESIGNS

PLATE 27. Flag, detail. Full quilt shown on page 50.

The family of designs we call "fans" is large and varied. Fans, made of concentric arcs, have also been called, Baptist Fans, Methodist Fans, Shells, and Waves. One reason they have been so popular with quiltmakers is that fans follow the natural arc of one's arm. That is why the design is sometimes called "elbow quilting." We divide fans into two main types: those that are marked and those that are quilted freehand. As the majority of fan designs are marked, we will start with those.

Small fans can be drafted with a simple drafting compass, but larger ones call for another tool. In our quest for homemade gadgets using inexpensive materials, we have designed a fan-maker.

It is a strip of single-layer cardboard, such as posterboard, about 2" x 18" with holes every ½" down the middle (*Figure 74*). The holes need only be large enough to allow a pencil point through. You use the fan-maker to make arcs by anchoring one end with a thumb tack through the first hole and a pencil point through the next one. Swing the pencil to make a perfect arc. Move the pencil to the next hole and repeat.

Start with a large piece of paper. Draw a line across it 5" from the long edge. To start these exercises we will give instructions for a compass. The principles will be exactly the same for using a fan-maker. To use a compass it is easiest to have a ruler handy. It is much quicker

Figure 74

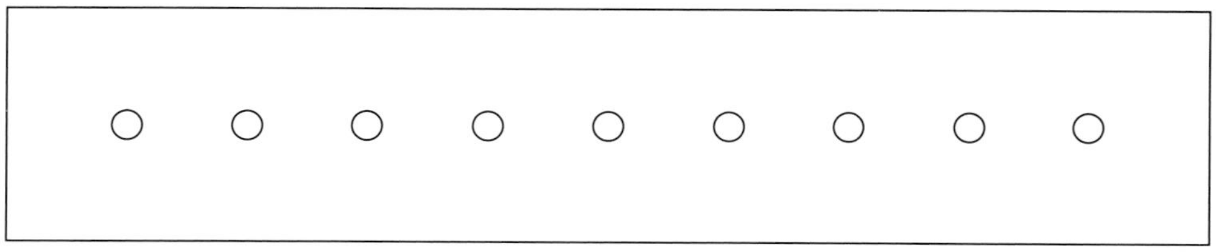

Figure 75

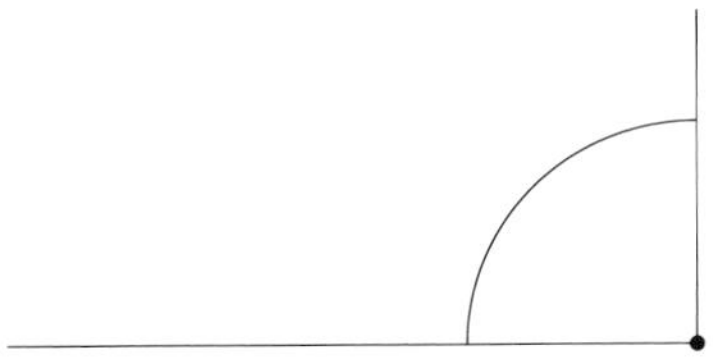

Figure 76

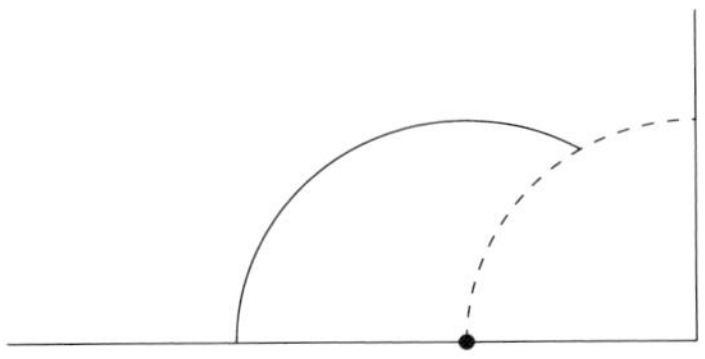

Figure 77

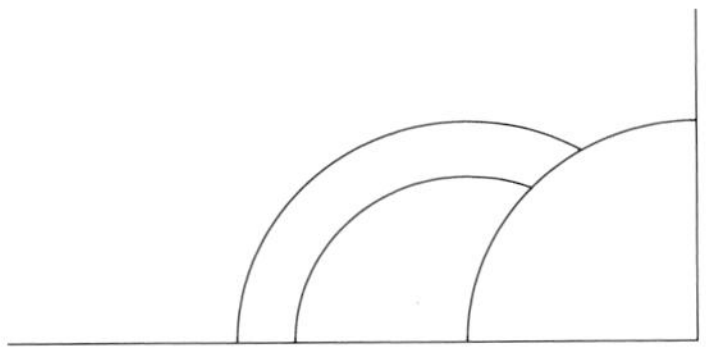

Figure 78

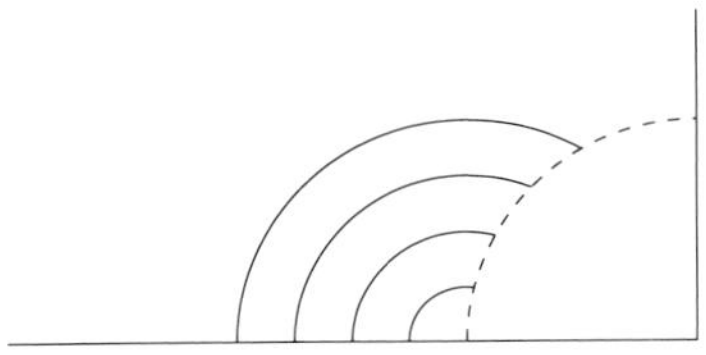

Figure 79

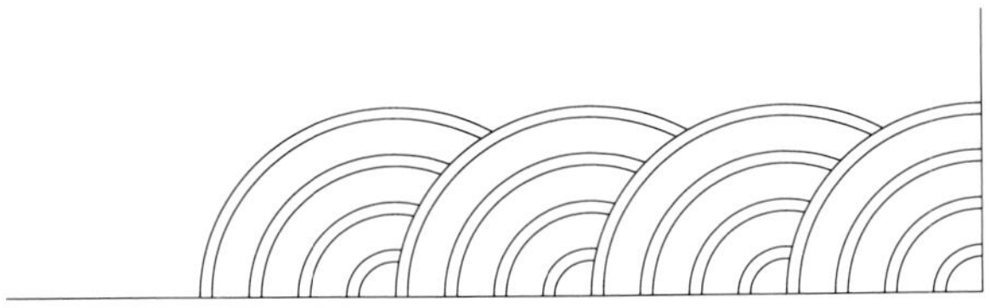

Figure 80

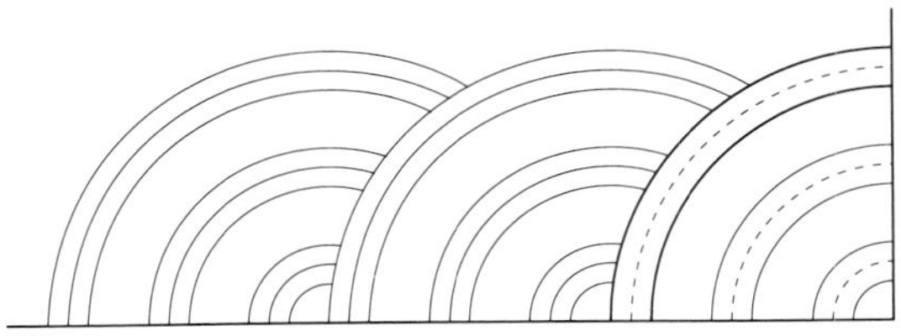

and more accurate to open or close the legs of the compass against a ruler than it is to try to read and use the small numbers etched on some inexpensive drafting compasses.

Open the compass to 4" and place the point on the line near the right edge of the paper, on the dot in *Figure 75*. Make a 4" arc as shown. This is your guide arc. Now, put the compass point at the base of the guide arc – on the dot as shown in *Figure 76* – and mark another 4" arc.

Close the compass to 3", keep the point in the same place and mark a second arc *(Figure 77)*. Mark two more arcs, at 2" and 1" *(Figure 78)*.

Now you have one fan unit that should look like ours. You no longer need the guide arc. Darken the arcs with a pen so you can trace the unit onto paper or fabric.

We think it is easiest to mark a line of fan units on paper, then trace the whole line onto the quilt top. With most fabrics this will require a light table. See the chapter on marking tools for instructions on how to set one up.

Fans can be doubled like most quilting designs *(Figure 79)*. As usual, we prefer to mark only the first lines, and to quilt the others freehand. They can be tripled the same way, but a more common way of tripling fans is to put a new line halfway between every other arc. This works best for fans with six or more arcs *(Figure 80)*.

There can be any number of arcs in a fan unit, and they can be spaced any way you like. Most compasses will not work for units larger than 6" or 7". For these large fans a fan-maker is the best tool.

We mark our fans from right to left, because that is the natural way for right-handed quilters like ourselves to quilt them in the frame. These are awkward for left-handed quilters. They should draft the units from left to right.

PLATE 28. Churn Dash, 62" x 72", 1989. Made by Gwen Marston.
We think that scrappy, loosely organized quilts like this call for informal, spontaneous quilting. Nothing could be less formal than freehand quilted fans. Notice the fans meeting and changing direction in the middle. It is remarkable how many old-time quilters employed this freehand-fan technique, and how few modern quilters do. It has fallen into obscurity mostly because it does not fit with the way we are taught to make quilts today. We are taught that the quilting should defer to the piecing.

BORDERS

When fans are used on borders there is usually a starting corner, where the first fan is exactly one quarter circle *(Figure 81)*. The usual method from there on is to have the fans run clear to the next corner, ending with a partial fan unit. The next border is built right against the end of the first one *(Figure 82)*. This is continued for all four sides *(Figure 83)*.

Small fans with diagonal lines can be used on wide borders like this *(Figure 84)*. You will recognize the idea from our discussion of clamshells earlier.

ALL-OVER

All-over fans were common until about the turn of this century. In the South, they seem to have been one of the most popular of all quilting designs, and they continue to be used there today.

Because of the nature of quilting during this revival, however, all-over fans have been little-used by the majority of modern quilters. The idea of quilting right across piecing or appliqué lines is antithetical to the idea that quilting should be subservient to piecing or appliqué.

We enjoy the idea of the quilting leading its own life, separate from the graphic design of the quilt. Studying old quilts, we have found hundreds of examples of quilting that seems to ignore the color design of the quilt. It is only because this approach is out of fashion at the moment that it is so seldom done. We often quilt all-over fans on our informal pieced or appliquéd quilt tops made of scraps. It worked in the past, and we think it still works well, as on Gwen's CHURN DASH *(Plate 28)*.

The fans can be marked in a number of ways, depending on the type of frame or hoop in which they will be quilted. If you quilt in a hoop or rectangular frame, a logical way to position the fans is to stack them from the bottom up, as we did

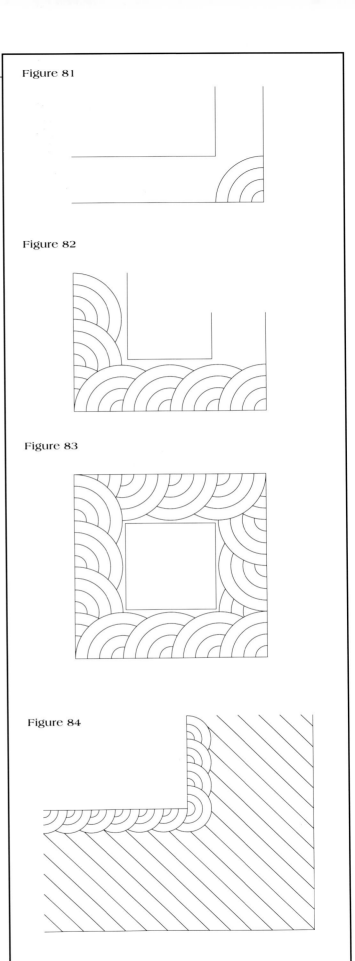

Figure 81

Figure 82

Figure 83

Figure 84

PLATE 29. Flag, 61" x 77", 1985. Made by the authors. Private Collection.
Here, as elsewhere, we wanted to use traditional patterns on a modern quilt. The field
of stars has all-over fan quilting, which was marked so as to be regular and symmetrical. The stripes have various feathers.

on the blue field of our FLAG in *Plate 29*, page 50. Once again, they should face to the right if you are right-handed and the opposite way if you are left-handed.

For full-frame quilters, who quilt from the outside in, the natural way to work is to first stitch a row of fans all the way around the outside. *(Figure 85)* Then rows can be filled in from each end, or side, toward the middle. Where the two sides meet, the odd space is usually filled in with partial fans *(Plate 30)*. You can use the same layout if you quilt in a hoop.

If you mark the fans from the bottom up and intend to quilt in a frame, just remember that you will often be quilting in an uncomfortable direction.

We have done this ourselves, however, when we wanted a certain effect. Our FLAG quilt, in *Plate 29*, has a large field of vertical fans. And our SNOWBALL quilt, in *Plate 20*, page 34, has fans moving in every direction. Sometimes it is worth a little tough quilting to say what you want.

PLATE 30. Gwen's Four Patch, detail. Full quilt shown on page 53.

FREEHAND FANS

The first time we sat down to quilt freehand fans on an unmarked quilt top, we were intimidated. What if our lines were not perfectly circular? What would happen when we met in the middle? What if we got mixed up and made some fans of six arcs and some of seven? What if we could not keep the spaces between the lines even? These and other questions made us wonder if we had made a mistake. Soon we realized we were worrying for nothing. Today, freehand fans is one of our favorite ways to quilt.

We studied many old quilts that were done this way in an attempt to learn the best approach. What we saw made us realize that there were not only a multitude of approaches, but there seemed in fact to be no rules at all. Some quilts had miniature fans going in every direction, some had large fans, 20" across. Some had a row all around the quilt, some had fans facing off from two sides. Some fans were quite circular, some looked like stair steps, or shelves. At our house we call those Shelf Fans *(Figure 86)*.

In nearly every case, we saw that the details mattered less than the overall effect of the design. In other words, it does not matter where or how you start

Figure 85

Figure 86

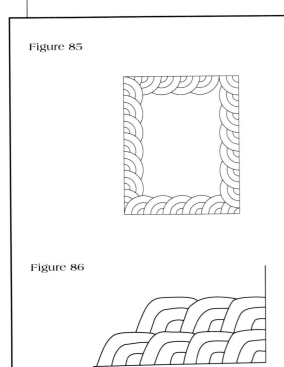

and stop each unit. It does not matter if some units have more arcs than others. It does not much matter how you fill in the extra space where the two sides meet in the middle.

In other words, freehand fans could take any size or shape we wanted. It was up to us to figure out how and where to start and stop.

Since we can only comfortably quilt 8" to 10" at a time in the frame, we decided to make the units only 7" tall. Not wanting to measure distances, we decided to make each arc about one needle length from the next. For the overall layout, we decided to quilt a row all the way around and then quilt rows from right to left from each end until we met in the middle. This is the system we used on CHURN DASH (Plate 28, page 48).

Once we had a feeling for how freehand fans looked, we tried them. For us the easiest way was to start with the smallest arc and build the first fan unit. We could just cut our thread long enough for two arcs, quilt the first one, thread the other end of the thread on the needle, skip up between the layers one needle length and quilt the next arc. At first it can be hard to make a smooth arc, but with a little practice your arcs will improve and become more circular.

The idea with freehand fans, as with any other freehand design, is that they will not be perfectly circular. The variations among individual fans and their spontaneity are what give them character. We have had many quilters tell us that, with our years of experience, it was easy for us to talk about how simple this could be, but they could never hope to get acceptable results with this technique. Yet, when we teach freehand fans at quilting retreats, everyone who tries becomes proficient after executing only one or two fan units.

We do not mean to imply that you should try to make the fans misshapen and "folksy," just the opposite. You should try to make them all the same size and shape, and accept the inevitable variations. Look at old quilts! A scrap quilt with a great deal of randomness and variation in the piecing does not necessarily call for machine-stamped quilting designs. Freehand fans are often more in character with these kinds of quilts, such as CHURN DASH (Plate 28, page 48) and GWEN'S FOUR PATCH (Plate 31).

GROUP QUILTING FANS

We think one of the main reasons fans are so often seen on old quilts is that they did not have to be marked before the top was put in the frame. It was especially handy at quilting bees to be able to put another top in as soon as the first one was done.

Everyone cannot just start in anywhere, though. Each quilter needs to know where the person on each side will start and stop. At our annual Beaver Island Quilt Retreat we have a quilt in the frame. We use it to teach the quilting stitch, and for a place for everyone to meet and visit. In 1989 we put in a top that we wanted to have everyone quilt with freehand fans. To get started, we made some cardboard templates the shape of a complete fan unit (Figure 87). With them we could mark all the outside fans so everyone would know where to start (Figure 88). Then they could fill in the rest of the units freehand.

The lines can be drawn with a marking tool, or they can even be scratched with a needle if the quilting is going to take place immediately. Once the first row is quilted all the way around, the quilt can be rolled and the second row on each end can be marked and quilted. See the section on frame quilting for more details.

PLATE 31. Gwen's Four Patch, 62" x 72", 1991. Made by Gwen Marston.
This scrap quilt, unlike some of ours, has a fairly structured block arrangement.
Still, it seemed to us that it called for the kind of quilting typical of scrap quilts
from the last century – all-over fans. Notice how the fans first are worked all the
way around the quilt then inward from two sides. Near the middle they just
collide.

Figure 87

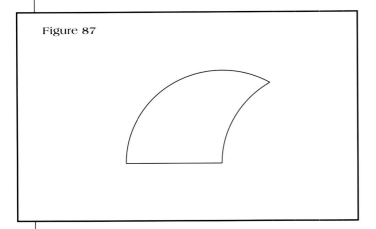

Figure 88

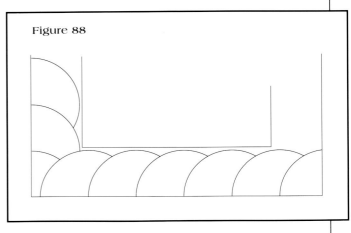

VARIATIONS

Some quilters use a fan variation based on a half-circle instead of a quarter-circle *(Figure 89)*. We have seen this on Amish, English and other quilts. With these half-circles, corner and middle resolutions can be fairly straightforward, because the arcs can intersect, or spaces left between them can be easily filled with partial circles. Draft these with a compass, as with the ones discussed earlier. The design can be varied by changing how much the units overlap, as in *Figures 90 and 91*.

If the half-circles are "squeezed" a bit, the resulting unit looks like *Figure 92*. We do not know the name of this design, but, because it reminds us of gothic arches, we call it, Gothic Fans. These can be used as part of a large design or as a border pattern *(Figure 93)*.

For us, the easiest way to draft these is to sketch the largest arch against the fold of a piece of paper, then use a ruler to make dots about ¾" inside it for the next one *(Figure 94)*. We fill in the smaller arches the same way. When we have one half of the design, we just hold the

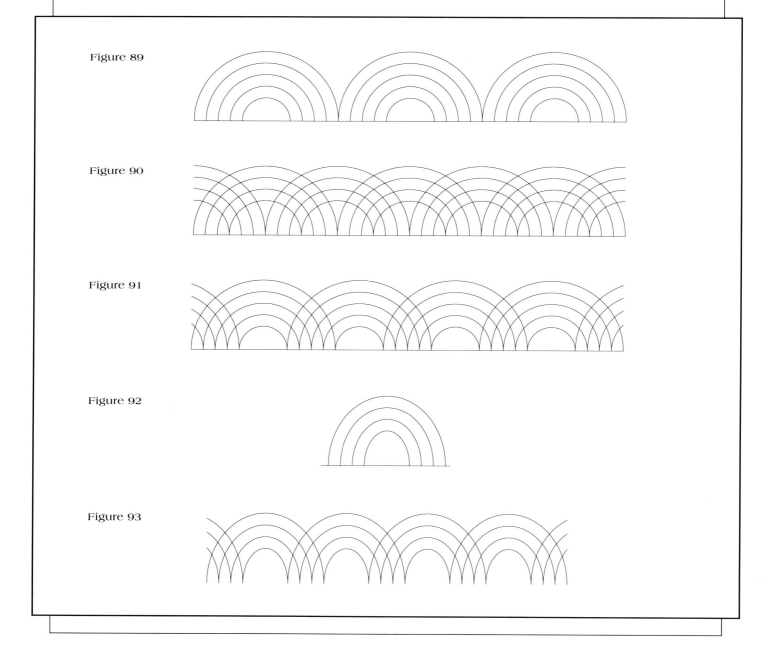

Figure 89

Figure 90

Figure 91

Figure 92

Figure 93

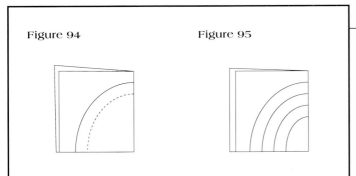

Figure 94   Figure 95

paper up to a window and trace it onto the other side *(Figure 95)*.

Depending upon how much room there is inside the unit, these can be overlapped in several ways. Try lining up the smallest arch of the first unit with the largest arch of the second unit as in *Figure 93*. Variously shaped arches produce different effects. If they are more "Gothic," or if the legs are straighter, the design will look like that in *Figure 96*. If the arches are spread more, the design will look more like *Figure 97*.

In general, we like to mark these from the middle of a border outward to the corners. Here you get the chance to start either in the middle of a unit or at the end of a unit at the middle of the quilt, whichever way works out best at the corners. If you want to resolve the corners symmetrically, you will probably need to design corner units. One possibility is a set of arches spread apart or closed together in such a way as to line up with those on both sides of the corner *(Figure 98)*. Another would be to put something completely different in the corners. Of course, you could work the other way around; start in the corners and work toward the middle. If the design does not work out as you like, you will need to design a middle resolution *(Figure 99)*.

However you use the Gothic Fan, it makes an elegant, formal design. Historically, these are most often seen on English and Welsh whole-cloth or "strippy" quilts. Nevertheless, the design lends itself well to modern quilts, and could be used in many settings. See the pattern section for a full-size Gothic Fan pattern.

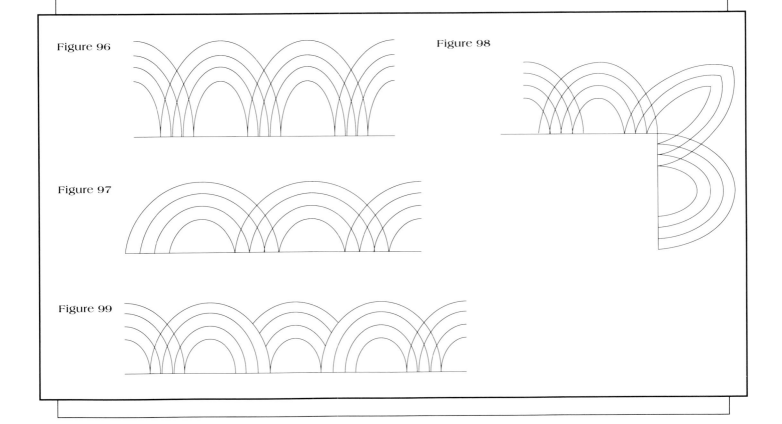

Figure 96

Figure 98

Figure 97

Figure 99

CABLE DESIGNS

PLATE 32. Variable Star Medallion, back, detail. Full quilt shown on page 69.

Most cable designs seem to be derived from the ancient braid or rope patterns seen in the folk art of many cultures. In quilts of the last century we see free, loose cables that seem to have been marked freehand, but these virtually disappeared with the widespread availability of commercial patterns. Now it seems that the quilters we meet think that cables are so difficult to draft that the only way to get one for a quilt is to buy it.

Actually, we used to think the same. However, once we found ourselves on a remote island and in need of a cable for a quilt top, we discovered that cables are really not so hard to design at all. In fact, we soon found ourselves designing new cables for any size border we had to work with, and the designs that had previously seemed hopelessly complex began to seem simple.

While there are many variations on the cable theme, quilters have used two basic types: one based on a football shape, and one based on the fan. Let's start with the simplest single football cable.

SINGLE CABLES

Cut a piece of paper into a small rectangle, 1¾" x 3". Now, fold it in half, and in half again. Make two marks on the folds as shown in *Figure 100*: ¼" up the short side from the folded corner, and ¾" over on the long side. Use your scissors to cut a curve from the long corner to the short corner and, parallel to it, from the long mark to the short one, as in *Figure 101*. (This is all much easier done than said.)

Unfold the paper, and you should have a football with a hole in the middle. If you have something different, try it again. The idea is to get a symmetrical, hollow shape like that shown in *Figure 102*. This is the football we will use in all the following exercises.

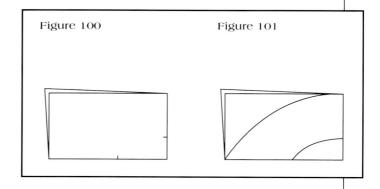

Figure 100   Figure 101

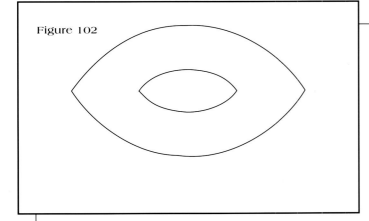

Figure 102

The easiest way to work with your football and make some single cable variations is to have a centerline to keep the points aligned. Draw a line on a piece of typing paper, a few inches down from the top edge. Make a few more center-lines while you are at it, each one 3" below the previous one. We will give you a variation for each line. In our drawings, the centerline is shown as a dotted line.

Just trace around the footballs, end to end. This is not exactly a cable, but it is a good place to start (Figure 103).

Start as above, but put the point of the second football against the inside point of the first one. This is a cable, a single cable (Figure 104).

Do this again, with a pencil. Now, erase the crossing lines as indicated by the dotted lines on the left. This makes the cable look more three dimensional (Figure 105).

Cut a 1" square from a piece of paper to help with this one. First, trace around a football, then line up the square on the guideline, from corner to corner and trace around it. Then another football, another square, and so on (Figure 106).

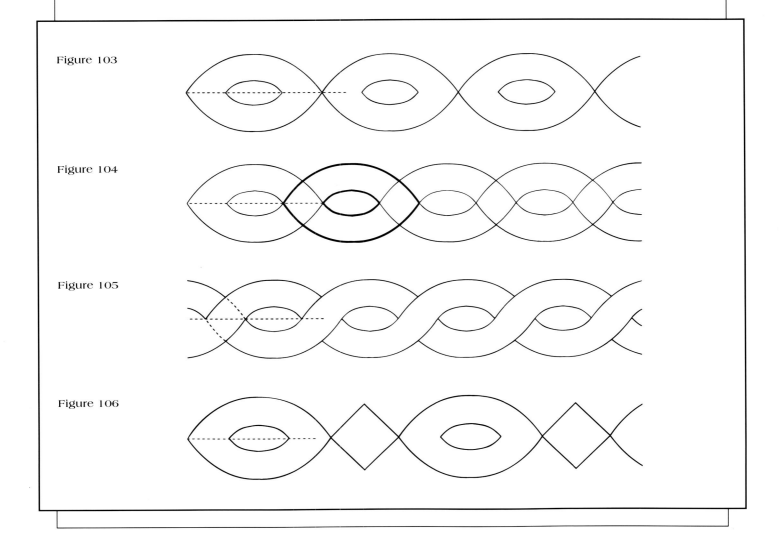

Figure 103

Figure 104

Figure 105

Figure 106

These designs are all good for narrow borders or lattice strips, 2¼" or a little larger. If your lattice or border is wider than that, you will probably want to make the football larger. In general, quilting designs should fill the space for which they are intended. On border designs like this, we like to keep the design ½" narrower than the border so we do not have to quilt through the seams.

If you want to design one of these for a specific border, just start out with a rectangle ½" less than the width of the border, to keep the cable out of the seams. In other words, if your border is 4" wide, start with a rectangle 3½" wide and as long as you want the unit to be. If you are not sure how long you want it, just cut one and lay it on the border to see how it looks. Do you want it longer? Do you want it shorter?

If you want the design to be absolutely symmetrical, cut a piece of paper one half the length of your border. Trace the cable on it, starting in the middle of the border and working toward the corner. If the last unit goes too far into the corner, try starting in the middle of a

unit to see how it would fit. If your cable is still too long or short, change the length of the unit accordingly.

Corners are simple with the football. If you want to make sure they will work out symmetrically, draw them on paper first. Put your guideline in the two borders that meet and start with a football in each direction (*Figure 107*). This design is short enough that you can easily shorten or lengthen some of them so they meet nicely in the middle of most borders. If you do not want to do this, simply make the rectangle from which you cut the original football a little longer or shorter, as you need it. Try it on paper again to see how it will work out.

This is not the only corner treatment. *Figure 108* shows the small inside footballs lined up at the corner and several lines erased to form a graceful corner resolution. In the past, many quilters simply ran two border designs edge to edge, then let the other two "collide" with them, as in *Figure 109*. Sometimes they would put another design altogether in the corner, as in *Figure 110*. There are many possibilities.

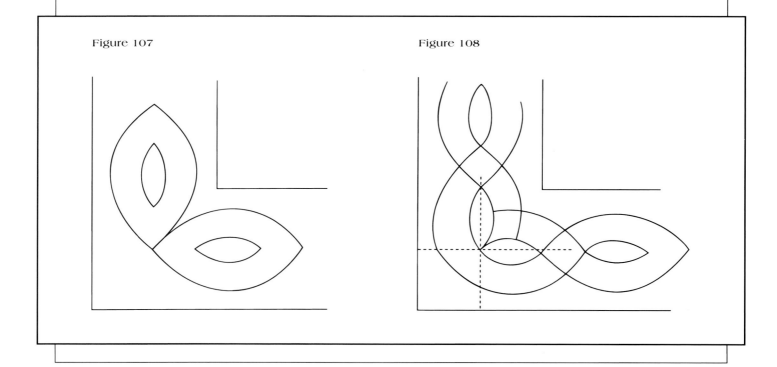

Figure 107

Figure 108

Figure 109

Figure 110

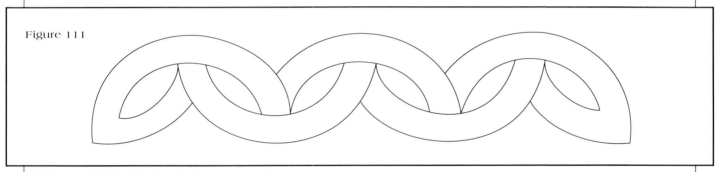

Figure 111

On your quilt top, you can either draw a light line for a guideline or press a line down the middle of your borders. If your border or lattice is light enough, you can make a section of the design on paper, slip it under the border and trace. If your fabric is too dark for this, just make your football out of cardboard and use it as a template on top.

At one of our Beaver Island Quilting Retreats a quilter named Carol Harris came up with the design in *Figure 111* using this same football shape. Try just playing with the shape to see what occurs to you.

The exact size and shape of this design does not matter, as long as the right end is the same length as the left

end. You can just fold a piece of paper twice, as we did at the beginning, and cut your football freehand. Try three or four of these, starting with different sizes of rectangles, and you will get the idea. Remember, you are making your own design, and the only "correct" one is the one that looks right to you.

MULTIPLE STRAND CABLES

Multiple-strand cables can be designed with the same football shape, with this added qualification: the horizontal measurements must be equal to each other, and the vertical measurements must be equal to each other. Take a look at *Figure 112*, page 60. The smallest, inside football shape, shown as the

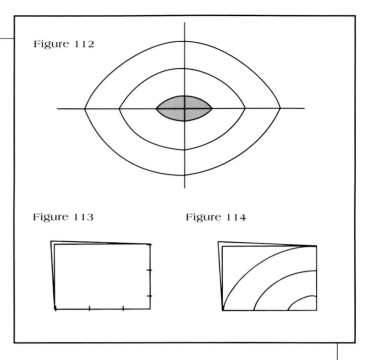

Figure 112

Figure 113   Figure 114

darkened area, is variable: it can be larger or smaller, as long as the rest of the measurements are equal. Thereafter, the horizontal measurements are all ⅝" and the vertical measurements are all ½". It is important to understand that these measurements are arbitrary. Different measurements simply result in a different cable. We could, for instance, lengthen the horizontal measurements, making a longer, flattened cable. As we proceed with our exercises this will become clear to you. For now, simply accept our measurements and work through the exercises with us.

In this lesson, we will design several cable variations for a 3" lattice. We will not outline the lattice, so our design should allow ¼" on both sides of the cable. Therefore, our cable should be 2½" thick.

Let's begin by cutting a rectangle 2½" x 3½". Fold this rectangle in half one way, and in half again the other way. Now you should have a rectangle that measures 1¼" x 1¾". Mark points vertically on the folded edge ¼", ½", and ½" apart. The horizontal marks are placed ½", ⅝" and ⅝" apart (*Figure 113*).

Sketch in curved lines connecting the points as shown in *Figure 114*. Cut along these lines and discard the center, the smallest football, shown as the darkened area. The remaining two football shapes will be used to create the following cable designs. These paper templates will work well enough to complete the following exercises as you learn the system.

However, when you are ready to use them to mark your quilt you will want to transfer them to cardboard or plastic for a more substantial and reliable template. When you transfer them to cardboard or plastic you may need to use a craft knife to cut out the smallest, center shape.

Because it is important to keep the cable design straight as it progresses, we will begin our first exercise by drawing a center line upon which to line up the end points of the football shapes. Draw around both the larger and smaller footballs as in *Figure 115*. Now line up the left point of the larger football with the right inner, smallest football shape of the first unit and draw around it. Complete this second unit by drawing around the smaller template (*Figure 116*). Continue in this way to complete the design shown in *Figure 117*.

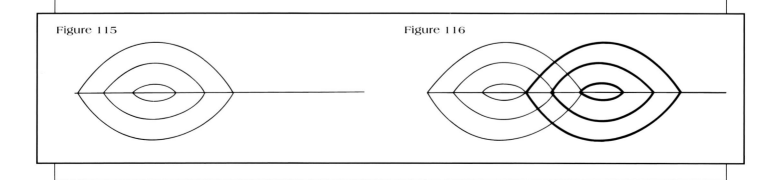

Figure 115

Figure 116

CABLE VARIATIONS

The following designs are created by eliminating certain lines to produce a different design. The lines to be eliminated are indicated by dotted lines.

In *Figure 118* the lines going in the same direction are eliminated at the intersections, producing the effect of an under/over pattern.

Figure 119 shows a more complex pattern created by erasing every other line in the outer square that is formed at the intersection. You can see this clearly in *Figure 120*. Look at the outside square that is formed at the junction of the cable units. You can start at any point and erase every other line of the square, producing the braided or woven effect.

Figure 121 has another set of lines erased. The result is that one part of the cable seems always to be in front of the other.

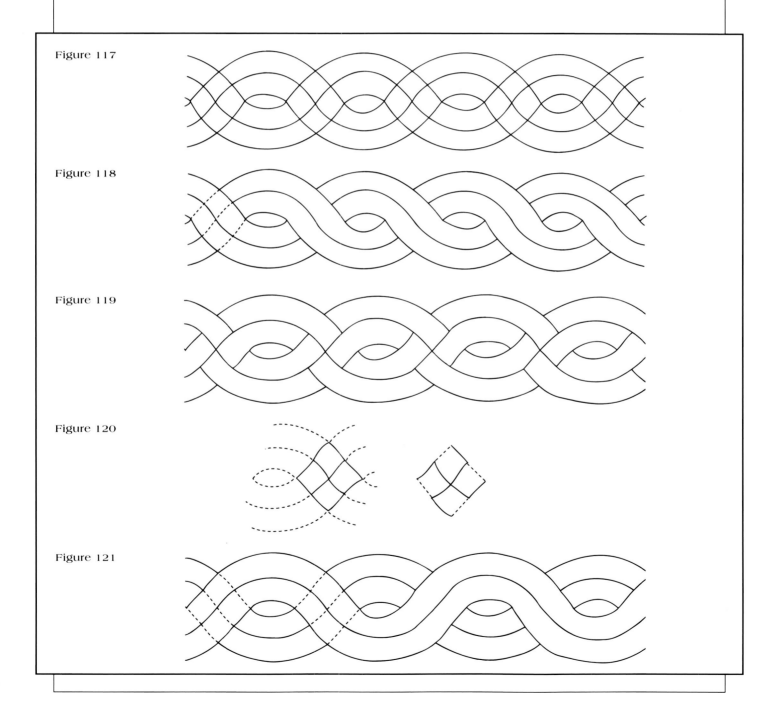

Figure 117

Figure 118

Figure 119

Figure 120

Figure 121

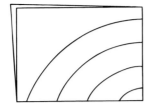

Figure 122

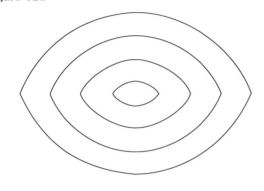

Figure 123

As with the single football designs, you can lengthen or shorten the units to adjust the length of the cable to fit your particular needs. Try folding another, larger rectangle and cutting more footballs. You will see the way that different curves and dimensions can alter the shape of the cable.

The basic method works to make cables with as many stands as you wish. Start out with a rectangle of paper, such as a piece of typing paper. Fold it in half, and in half again. Now, working from the corner that is all folds, measure and make marks in one direction ¼", then ½", ½", ½" apart. In the other direction, mark points ½", ⅝", ⅝", ⅝" apart. See *Figure 122* to connect the dots with curves and cut out the footballs. Discard the small, solid one and the outer piece of scrap paper. This many footballs will make a three-strand cable. No matter how many you are working with, however, the system is always the same: draft one complete football unit, of as many strands as you

like *(Figure 123)*. Line up the smallest unit on a center line and trace around it, inside and out. Begin the second unit by placing the left point of the largest football shape at the right point of the inner, smallest football shape and tracing around it, completing the unit and continuing in this fashion to complete the cable *(Figure 124)*.

Erase one set of lines, as in *Figure 125*, to get a variation we have seen on borders of Midwest Amish Quilts *(Figure 126)*. *Figures 127 and 128* are two variations of a five-strand cable, designed using the same principles.

Remember that the system is always the same. The number of strands and the measurements themselves are variable, as long as the measurements from point to point are equal. You will want to experiment with different measurements to see the difference and then determine for yourself what shape you like best. There is no "correct" shape, no definitive formula, only a system.

Now that you know how to draft cables the next question is how to resolve corners when using them. Resolving corners on cable designs is probably more difficult than with any other design because there are so many variables: the number of strands, width and length of borders, etc. Cables, however, are an ancient design used by Greeks, Romans, and Egyptians. When we travel on our lecture tours, we always try to visit the local art museums and see what they have in the way of antiquities. We have found that early craftsmen resolved cable designs by either shortening or lengthening several units. This is not called "cheating"; it is called "designing." It is one way of resolving the cable design.

Another way is to draft a cable design to fit one half of the border of your quilt. Try lining it up on the midpoint of the

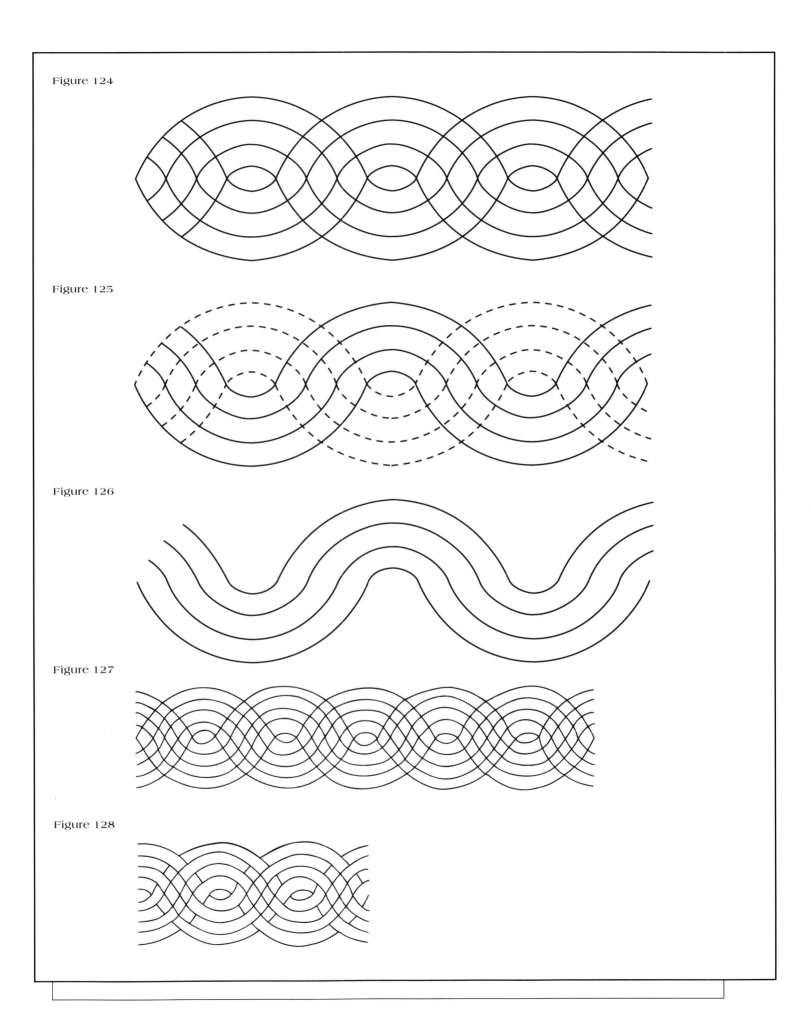

Figure 124

Figure 125

Figure 126

Figure 127

Figure 128

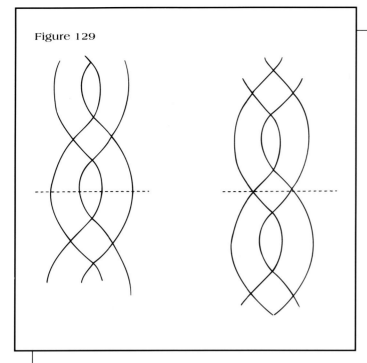

Figure 129

border, starting first at the intersection of the units, then at the middle of the units, to see how this will affect the corners (*Figure 129*). In this way you can tell exactly what adjustments you need to make. You may want to make your unit a little bit longer or shorter, to make it land where you want in the corner. You can also follow the lead of the old craftspeople and make minor adjustments in the length of a few units at any point along the side of the border.

For working on long designs like this, we buy butcher paper from our local butcher. You can also use shelf paper, rolls of scrap newsprint, or any kind of paper you can find of the necessary length. We like butcher paper because we can see through it enough to trace designs easily.

On to the corners! *Figures 130, 131, 132, and 133* show some possible corner treatments. *Figures 132 and 133* are perhaps the most flexible, because they can quite easily be stretched or shrunk, depending on where the last units end up in the corner.

Another common corner on early quilts was the "collision" corner. To create this, simply run the cable right off the ends of two borders and butt the other sides right up against them as in *Figure 134*. This is a great idea if you are making an old-fashioned quilt. Many quilters like to make new quilt tops that look like old ones. But when it comes to the quilting designs, fewer follow the old methods. The collision corner seems especially appropriate for this kind of quilt – given that the majority of cables on old quilts used it.

No single corner resolution is right for every single quilt. Think about the quilt for which your cable is being designed. Is it tightly controlled and formal? Is it looser and scrappy?

When we mark two or three-strand cables on our quilt tops, it seems easiest for us to use the football templates themselves. For many-strand cables it seems easier to draft a section of the design and trace it on the quilt.

FAN-BASED CABLES

An entirely different cable is based on the fan. We call this design a "classical" cable. As with many designs, we think of it as belonging to the tradition of quilting, but it is a design that has been used by craftspersons all over the world for centuries. It is part of an ancient design vocabulary known to the Greeks, Etruscans, Egyptians, and Romans, as well as to craftspersons in Oriental and many other early civilizations. It has been used to decorate buildings, pottery and mosaics. It was also used as a decorative pattern by woodcarvers on furniture and doors. American quilters may have appropriated it from the popular neoclassical buildings of the 1770's, but we really do not know how or when it was first used on quilts.

The first step in drafting this design is to draw a guide line the long way across the middle of a piece of typing paper.

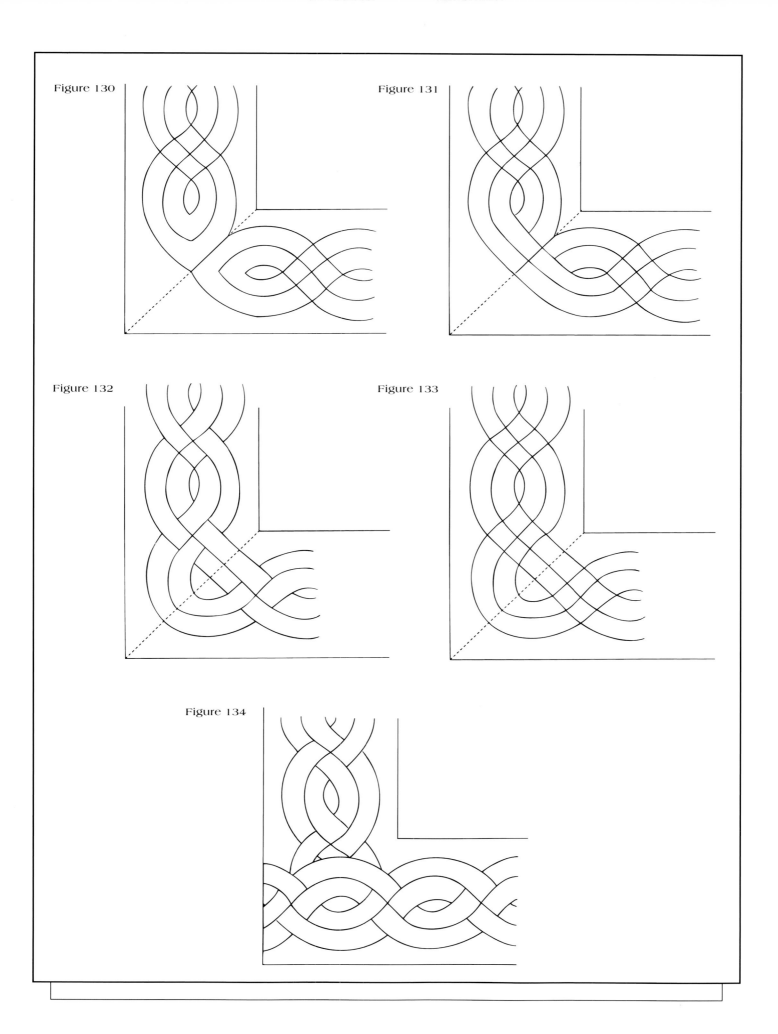

Figure 130

Figure 131

Figure 132

Figure 133

Figure 134

Set your compass at 2½", place the point of the compass on the guide line at the right edge of the paper and draw an arc. Now measure a series of five ½" increments on the guide line beyond this first arc (Figure 135).

Leave your compass set the same as above and make another arc beside the first one, starting with the point where the first one meets the guide line. Now, close the compass to the next smaller mark and make the next arc. Repeat this process to draw in the remaining arcs, always leaving the point of the compass at the base of the first arc which is indicated by a dot (Figure 136). It is this second unit with which we will draft our cable. The first large arc simply serves as a guide for determining the correct length of the curved lines in the second unit. In other words, we can now ignore the first large arc.

Draw a guideline down the middle of a piece of tracing paper. Line up the guidelines on both sheets of paper and trace the fan so that it is resting on the guideline. Trace the fan on the tracing paper, then rotate the tracing paper and place the fan *below* the guideline. Line up the smallest arc on the tracing paper with the largest arc on the bottom paper and trace the design again as shown in Figure 137. Now you have a complete segment of the cable design. Darken in the design with a black felt-tip pen so that it will be easy to trace for the next step.

Using the completed segment you can now draft a section of the classical cable shown in Figure 138. To draft a longer section of the cable you will want to use a large sheet of paper such as butcher paper or shelf paper. Draw a horizontal line across the paper, about 3" or 4" down from one edge. It is always important to have this center guideline to insure that the design develops

consistently and remains straight as each segment is added. Line up the guide lines and trace the unit once. Now move it along the guideline and trace it repeatedly to create the cable design.

You will notice the center shape of our design is oblong. Experiment with this design by shifting the unit a little closer to the previous unit. By making a few adjustments you can draft a design that has a circle in the middle rather than an oblong. Again, we remind you that this is a system, not a formula, and you will need to play around with it to see how it works. The number of strands you make and the measurements between the arcs are both variable. Try drafting a five-strand cable with arcs 1" apart for a wide border.

As we mentioned, an old-fashioned method of handling the corners was simply to run the cables clear to the ends of the first two borders and butt the adjoining cables up against them. However, if you want your border designs to be symmetrical in all four corners here are two ways to accomplish it. The first method is to mark all four corners by extending the curved lines to form a circle as shown in Figure 139. Do the corners like this before you do the borders. Then fill in the cables along each side of the border and it will automatically feed into the circle. We used this method on our TULIP AND OAK LEAF quilt, shown in our book *American Beauties* (Plate 38, page 38) and also on page 68 of this book.

For the second method you can stretch or compress a few units slightly. By imperceptibly lengthening or shortening a few units of the cable on the outer border of our VARIABLE STAR MEDALLION (Plate 38, page 89), we made the corners work out symmetrically. Here, on the back of the quilt, it is easy to see how the diagonal corners match (Plate 34, page 69).

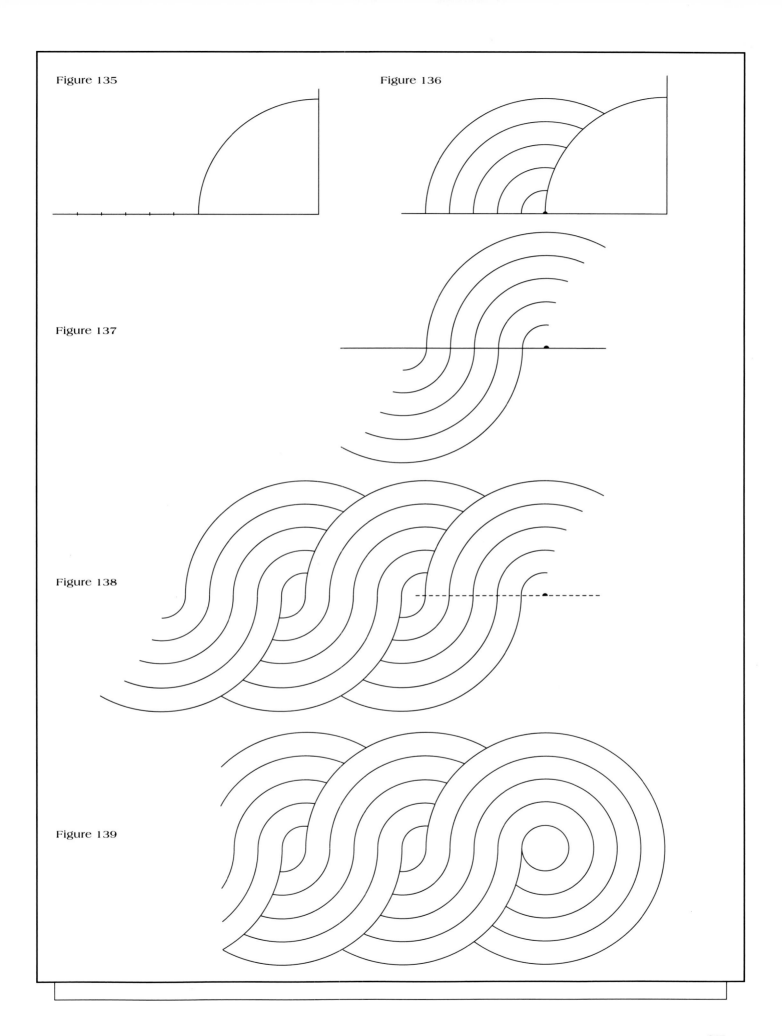

Figure 135

Figure 136

Figure 137

Figure 138

Figure 139

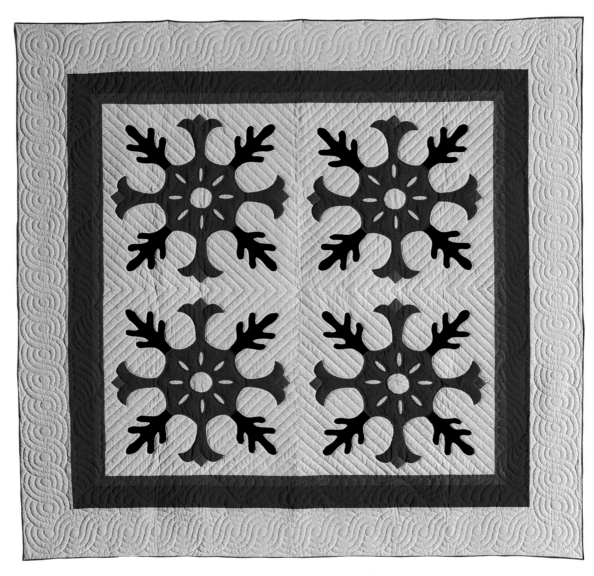

PLATE 33. Tulip and Oak Leaf, 75" x 75", 1987. Made by the authors.

PLATE 34. Variable Star Medallion, back, 82" x 88", 1981. Made by the authors.
The cable on the outer border has two different corner resolutions. By making slight alterations in the length of a few units we made the cables work out evenly at the corners. But, one side extended further into the corner than the other. Therefore, we needed to create the different resolutions.

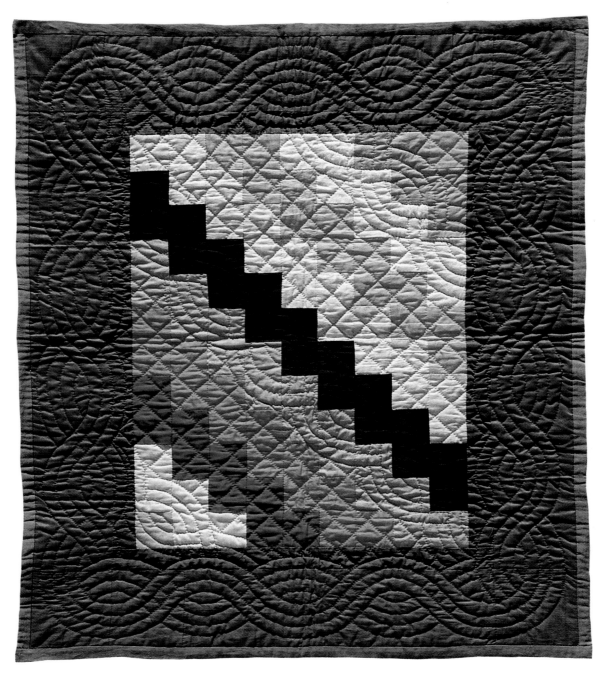

PLATE 35. Streak of Lightning, 30" x 36", 1983. Top made by Mary Schafer; quilted by the authors.
We like this unusual use of cables so well that we have repeated the theme in several quilts since.

Figure 140

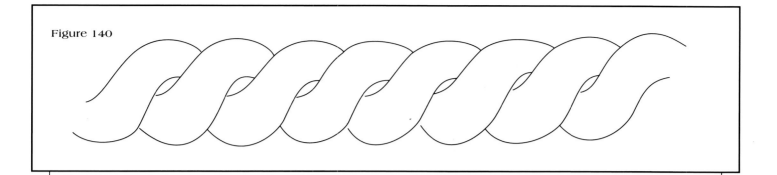

VARIATIONS

In *Figure 140* we show the actual size of a tiny cable which we used in a 1½" border on one of our doll quilts. It is often difficult to think of a quilting design for very narrow borders. This one works beautifully. As you can see, this design is made of just two arcs. Try drafting this cable for a 3" lattice.

Cable designs are most often used on borders or lattice, but we have seen them used in other ways, too. Mary Schafer made us a quilt top which was a copy of an early twentieth century Ohio Amish quilt. We decided to quilt it like the original. The border was quilted with a multiple-strand cable, which is a popular Amish border design. The interior section of the quilt, however, had an uncommon treatment. It had three multiple-strand cables running diagonally across it. The remaining areas were filled in with crosshatching *(Plate 35).*

We saw a delightful red and green four-block appliqué quilt from the turn of the century upon which the quilter had quilted wide multiple-strand cables horizontally from the top to the bottom of the quilt, right over the appliqué. The wide cables alternated with equally wide areas of crosshatching.

ALTERNATE METHODS AND PATTERNS FOR CABLES

Cable designs are popular in part because they are so flexible. You can easily devise your own variation on any of the classic cable themes. Here, we will give you some "starter" ideas and techniques.

First, we will show another way to draft a cable, based on yet a third technique: folded paper. We call this the "Paper Doll" cable. Start out with a piece of paper the length of a piece of typing paper and one third the width. Fold it in half, and in half again *(Figure 141).* Instead of cutting paper dolls holding hands, we are going to cut out a cable section. Sketch it on your paper as in *Figure 142.* In order to make it symmetrical, fold your paper in half side to side again, then top to bottom. Now you should have a small square with one fourth of your drawing showing, as in *Figure 143.*

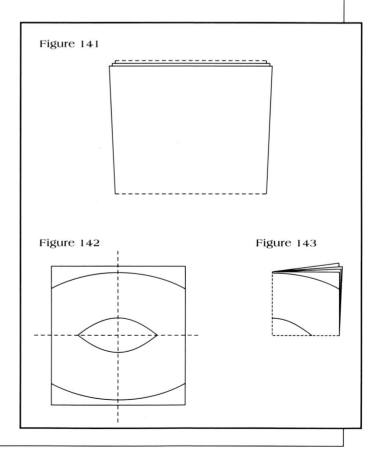

Figure 141

Figure 142

Figure 143

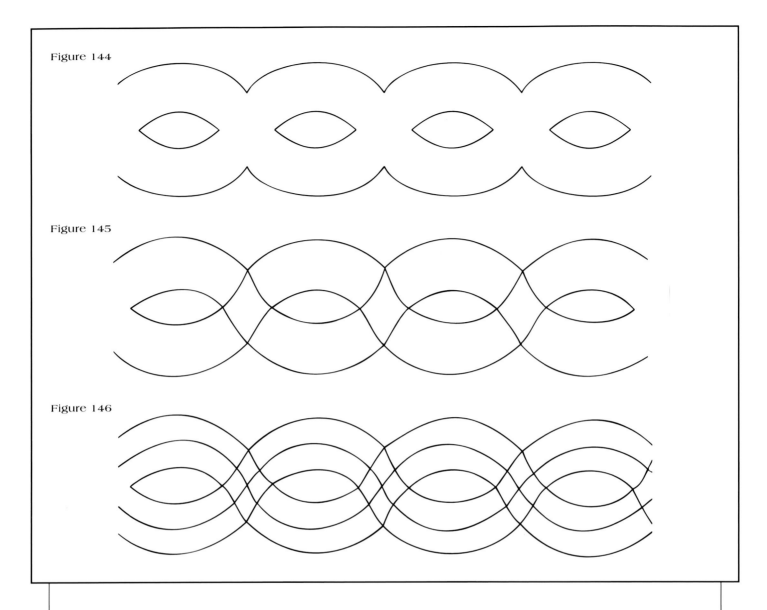

Figure 144

Figure 145

Figure 146

Cut on the lines and unfold the paper to get an outline of a cable (*Figure 144*).

For a cable this size you can just connect the inner and outer lines, as in *Figure 145*. Or, you could add another line down the middle of each side (*Figure 146*). All the principles we have discussed regarding the football cable would apply to this one as well.

A circular cable can be designed with another folded paper method. Start out with a fairly large circle of paper, 8" to 10". Fold it three times to make a cone as shown in *Figure 147*. Trim the corners of the top so it looks roughly like the one shown. When you unfold the paper you should have a shape like this

(*Figure 148*). If your curves are too deep or too shallow, just fold up the pattern again and trim it more to your liking. Then, draw in the fold lines for guides to the next steps. To make a circular cable, just follow three simple steps.

• First, echo the edge of the paper, ¼" inside (*Figure 149*).

• Second, draw an arc from point to point as shown in *Figure 150*.

• Third, connect the valleys with arcs (*Figure 151*). Your finished design can be filled with any designs from earlier exercises. Also, you can erase some of the crossing lines to get the same "over and under" effect as with other cables (*Figure 152*).

Figure 147

Figure 148

Figure 149

Figure 150

Figure 151

Figure 152

The technique described on pages 71 and 72 could be used with a larger piece of paper, perhaps folded one more time. If you are working with larger paper, you might have trouble folding it precisely if it is too thick. Thinner paper, such as tracing paper, is helpful for the accurate folding of large designs.

You can modify any football cable by making it of diamonds instead of footballs. Fold a piece of paper twice and cut it as shown in *Figure 153* to make a diamond. Here is how some single cables look when they are made using diamonds *(Figure 154)*. Double diamond cables look like the cable in *Figure 155*.

Figure 153　　　　　Figure 154

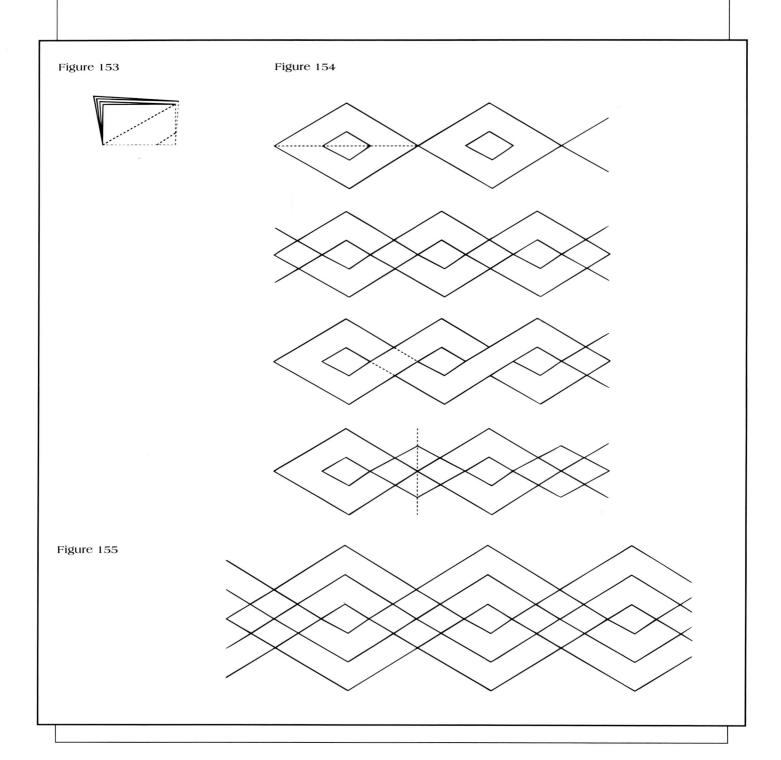

Figure 155

Make the diamond very thin and round off the top and bottom points and you will get the unit for another cable altogether *(Figure 156)*. Note that the ends of these units must overlap in the middle of the unit *(Figure 157)*. To make a variation we erased the dotted lines shown in *Figure 158*.

Use just the outside of a small football, lined up as indicated in the drawings, to make the variation shown in *Figure 159*.

For the next three variations we just combined the small football with a square. By changing the shapes of the footballs and squares you can make

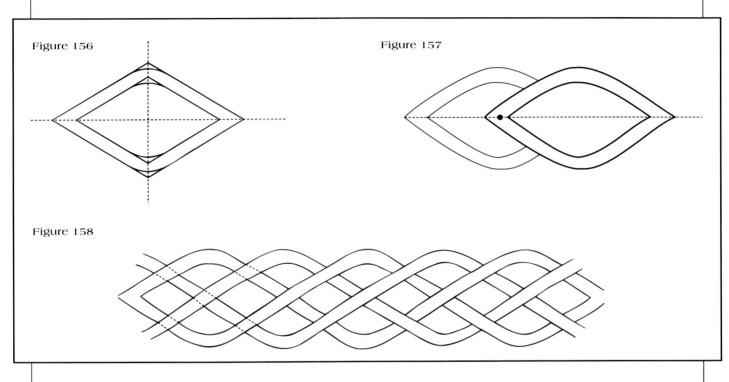

Figure 156

Figure 157

Figure 158

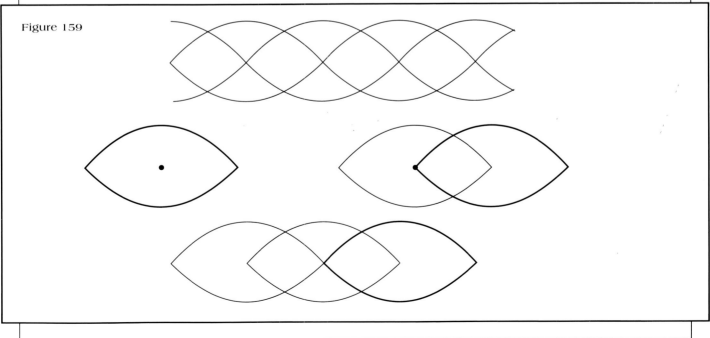

Figure 159

endless variations *(Figure 160)*.

    Figure 161 shows the single football from *Figure 103* and various square shapes at the intersections.

    You can even combine cables with feathers. Make a five-strand cable as in *Figure 138* and replace every other unit with feathers. Just keep the middle strand for a "spine" for the feathers, as shown in *Figure 162*. All you need now is to learn how to draw the feathers used. Stay tuned.

Figure 160

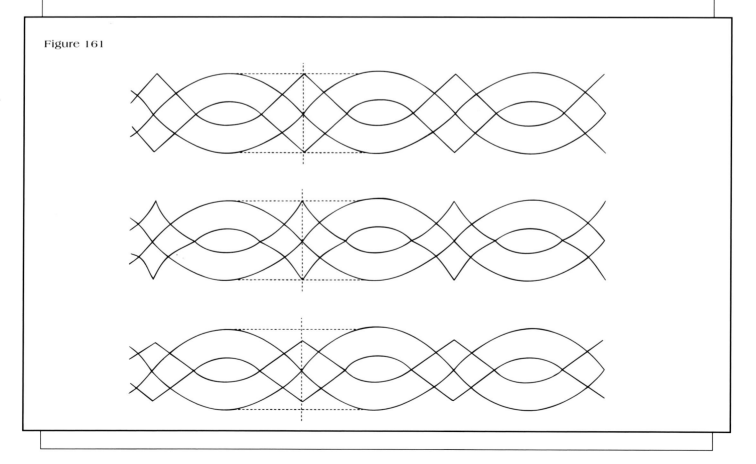

Figure 161

Figure 162

CHAPTER 6

FEATHER
DESIGNS

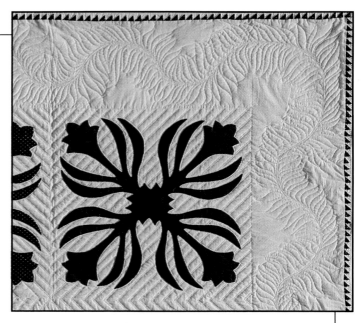

PLATE 36. Blue Tulip, detail. Full quilt shown on page 90.

Wwhile most of the patterns we have discussed up to now are often seen in other design traditions from various cultures, the family of designs called "Feathers" has been developed primarily by quilters for quilts. Feathers seem to have their origin in common medieval plume designs. Used on tapestries, embroideries, etchings, and prints, feathers originally seem to have been associated with royalty and elegance. Quilters have tended to use unique versions of them for showy, ambitious quilts. But feathers have also become a standard part of the quilting design repertoire and are seen on all kinds of quilts.

In our studies of these designs we have seen many kinds of feathers – short,

tall, fat, thin, slanted, and straight. In our time we have seen feathers become more homogeneous and standardized, a result of modern templates and teaching techniques. In previous times, however, feathers were more varied and individual; some were even quilted freehand! We have come to think that it is best to learn to draw feathers yourself, so you can make the different types for which different quilts call.

Most of our students resist the idea of "drawing." Marking feathers is not really drawing, though. It is more like learning to make a single new letter of the alphabet and doing it over and over. The feather design only has two basic parts: a line to which the feathers are attached,

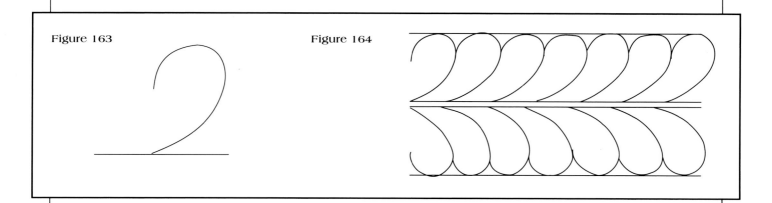

Figure 163

Figure 164

which we call the "spine," and the feather itself, a simple curve like that shown in *Figure 163*. You can learn to draw feathers with just a few minutes of practice.

Why do this at all, you might ask, when nearly every shop carries feather templates for the same purpose? There are several benefits of learning to draft your own. First, as we have said before, it is rare to find a template exactly the size and proportion that you need for a specific quilt. Second, your feathers will not look exactly like anyone else's, so you will have a chance to put your individual stamp on the quilting designs for your quilt. Third, and perhaps most important, it is *easier* and *faster* to mark feathers freehand on fabric than either tracing around a teardrop template or marking in the slots of a large feather pattern. Yes, that is what we said: *easier* and *faster*. Try it and see.

STRAIGHT FEATHERS

The simplest feather design is the straight feather *(Figure 164)*. It is a design that works well for either narrow borders or lattice strips. All the feathers lean in the same direction and at the same angle. The straight spine can be either single or double. We prefer the richer look of the double spine for nearly all our feather designs. We usually make the two lines slightly less than ¼" apart.

Start by using a ruler to make two parallel lines 3" apart. Then draw two

more lines between them for the spine, about ⅛" apart *(Figure 165)*. The outside lines are "limit" lines which make it easier to make your feathers all the same size.

An easy feather with which to start is a rounded, fairly plump one. It looks like the one in *Figure 164*. There are a few significant points to keep in mind when you practice drawing it. Always start from the top, at point A, and draw the cap, then draw downward to the spine *(Figure 166)*. Notice that the feather starts and stops against an imaginary vertical line. Also, it curves in one direction only, and keeps curving until it finally touches the spine. Do not let your feathers "recurve" as the one does in *Figure 167*. When you first try this, remember to make the feathers plump like the one shown.

Now, try making a few of these this size on a piece of scratch paper. Do not worry if they are not regular and exactly like ours. Just try to keep them curving in one direction, keep them plump, and keep them vertical. If you are having trouble and you are drawing very slowly, try drawing a little faster. If you are drawing quickly and still having trouble, try drawing more slowly. Also, do not sketch each feather with a series of short lines. Mark each one with a single line, deliberately and carefully, just as you would if you were making a letter of the alphabet.

Once you have drawn eight or ten practice feathers, try filling in the top row,

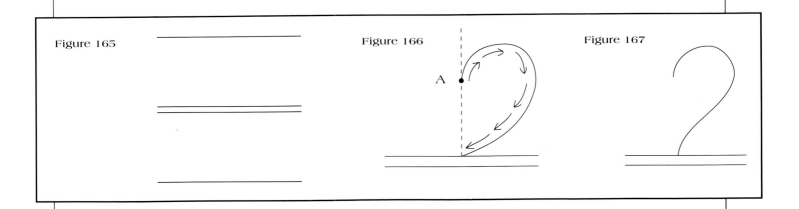

Figure 165

Figure 166

Figure 167

Figure 168

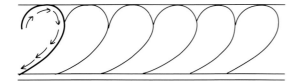

Figure 169

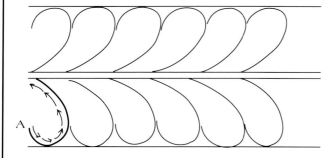

Figure 170

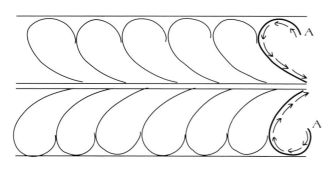

need to make feathers in all directions, and it is either awkward or impossible to keep turning the quilt top the way you need it. A few more minutes of practice now will pay off later. Some people even find this direction easier than the other. Once again, draw from point A to the spine, not the other way around *(Figure 169)*. Try a few of these.

You may have the urge to make the ends of the feathers touch in the middle, where they meet the spine. We think they look best if they do *not* meet in the middle. Look at *Figure 164* and see what you think. In any case, this straight feather is the only one where it is even possible to make them meet, as all curved feathers will have more feathers on the outside of the curve than the inside and trying to make them meet will lead to gross distortion of the design.

Fill in the bottom feathers. Take your time and ignore the top row. Just try to make feathers that are plump and even.

Now, make another setup of doubled spine and guidelines and try repeating the exercise from right to left. As with the bottom feathers, some people find this direction easier, some more difficult *(Figure 170)*. Always start at point A and mark the feather against the "shoulder" of the previous one. Do not start them against the spine, or out in mid air. Notice that we have darkened the first feather so you can see where to start.

Turning a corner with this straight feather can be done with a straightforward butt-joint *(Figure 171)*.

Alternatively, you could just end the feather and put another design altogether in the corner, such as a small feather wreath *(Figure 172)*.

Many quilters will want to make the feathers run smoothly around the corner. With this straight feather, that means truncating the last feather or two on the inside of the corner, as shown in *(Figure 173)*.

as in *Figure 168*. Start with the darkened feather. Do not worry if they are not exactly even and alike. Try to make them even. But do not erase or worry. After all, this is the first time you have tried this! If yours look a great deal different than ours, try to compare them and see why. Are yours thinner? Are they starting and stopping vertically? Are they curving in one direction?

Now, keep the paper in the same position and practice drawing the bottom feathers. Yes, you could just flip the paper and fill in the other ones...but when you are marking these on a quilt you will

Figure 171

Figure 172

Figure 173

VINES

After three or four practice runs through the straight feather exercise you will be ready to try a feather on a curved spine. Most feather designs are built this way. First you will need a curve. It is hard to just draw a symmetrical curve, but simple to draft one using our folded-paper method.

For this exercise, cut a strip of paper 6" x 24". Now, fold it in half, then in half again. The resulting square should be 6" x 6". The folds should be on the right and left sides.

On the right side, measure up 2" and make a pencil mark. On the other side, measure down 2" and make a pencil mark. Lay your ruler from one mark to the other and make a line *(Figure 174)*. You need one more mark – in the middle of the line. Find this by folding the square again and pinching the middle. Put the paper in front of you as in the drawing, with the high mark on the left and the low one on the right.

Use a pencil to sketch a rough curve like the one in *Figure 175*, one that starts on the top of the left mark, never gets more than about ¼" from the straight line, crosses at the midpoint, and repeats itself to the other mark. Just scribble with your pencil until you have a general curve that looks symmetrical, then darken it in. It should look like the drawing. Now, take your paper scissors and cut on

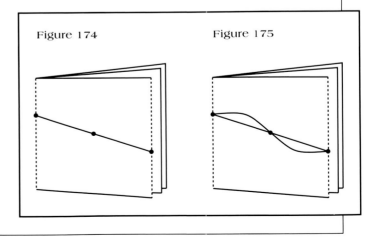

Figure 174   Figure 175

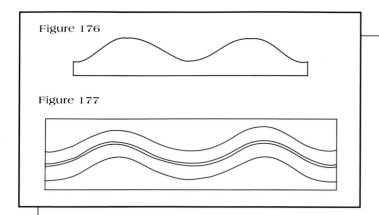

Figure 176

Figure 177

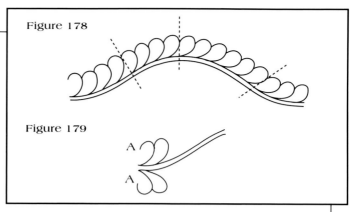

Figure 178

Figure 179

the curved line, through all the layers of the folded paper. When you unfold it, your curve should look more or less like the one in *Figure 176*.

This is your own pattern for a feathered vine. You can just transfer the curve to cloth – if you are ready to mark on fabric – or, for right now, to a large piece of paper. Once you have the curve, you can double it freehand with another curve a bit less than ¼" away.

When you have done this a few times, this is all you will need to make your feather design on your quilt. For now, however, it is best to have guidelines that will help you keep all the feathers the same height. The easiest way to mark these is with a compass. Open it up to 1½" and drag the point along the curve, allowing the pencil to make a line 1½" away. Repeat on the other curve. Now your setup should look like *Figure 177*.

Start your feathers in the same way and place as you did with the straight feather exercise. The only difference is that, while the feathers this time will stay basically perpendicular to the spine, they lean back and forth as the spine snakes around (*Figure 178*). Start from point A on the feathers and end up on the spine, not the other way around (*Figure 179*). Keep the feathers curving as they approach the spine. You may have a tendency to want to straighten them out to hit the spine more quickly...do not do that.

You may also find it a little difficult to keep them all the same height at first, but if you simply stay against the guideline all the way along you will soon get over that. The hardest point for most people seems to be the "valley" of the curve, where there are the fewest feathers and the longest curves. Study the drawing in *Figure 180* carefully to see what happens. Fill in the top row, then do the

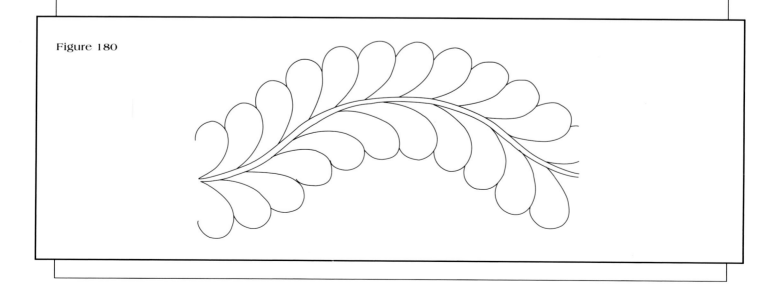

Figure 180

bottom feathers, just as in the drawing. Notice how the feathers do not line up – because there are more on the outside of the curves than the inside.

This seems like a lot to remember, doesn't it? Actually, if you try this two or three times, you will find it all becoming second nature. Once you feel comfortable going from right to left, work the other way, and make sure to reverse the feathers *(Figure 181)*. Spend a while filling a large piece of paper up with feathered curves and you will find yourself comfortable drawing the feathers in every direction.

Make sure the feathers on top of the curve and those on the bottom both curve the same way, as in *Figure 182*. They should not look like those in *Figure 183*. Remember, too, to always start the feather on the "shoulder" of the previous feather, as in *Figure 184*, not in mid-air as in *Figure 185*.

You can design a feathered vine like this for any size quilt. Just start with a piece of paper the same width as your border and either the same length or one half its length. That is, its length without the "corner squares" *(Figure 186)*. As you draft the curve, remember that the width of the completed design needs to be a little smaller than the border itself, so the feathers do not go clear to the seam line or the outer edge of the quilt. You do not want to quilt in the seam allowances and you will need room on the outer edge to add the binding.

Fold the paper in half, then in half again, and again, until the rectangle you have is a reasonable size for one unit of the curve. If the rectangle is too narrow, the curve will be too short and steep...if it is too wide, the curve may be too gentle. There is no rule for the proportions of the curve. You just need to do what we do when we design a curve: experiment. Cut one and see how it looks in the area it will fill. Once you have cut the final curve

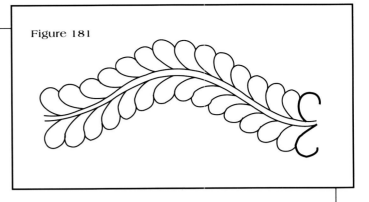

Figure 181

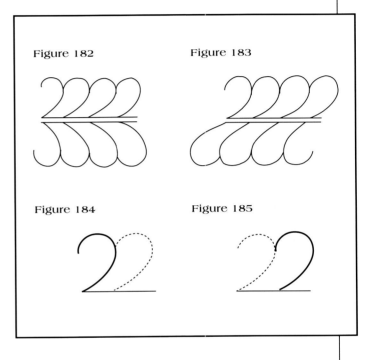

Figure 182   Figure 183

Figure 184   Figure 185

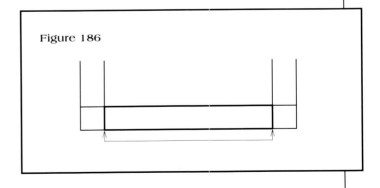

Figure 186

and unfolded it, notice that one curve ends up high and one low. The curve is the same, but the different ends will allow you to check how the curve will work with the corner square. Cut a piece of paper the size of your corner square.

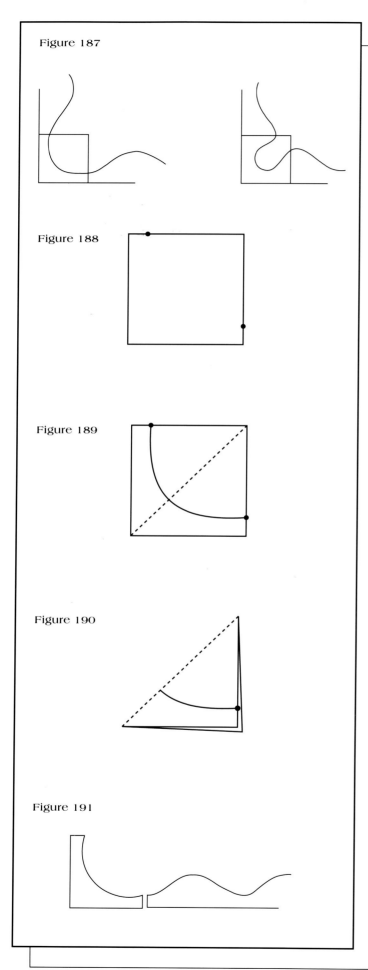

Figure 187

Figure 188

Figure 189

Figure 190

Figure 191

CORNERS

Now, decide which way you want the spine to enter the corner square. Will it look better to you if it enters the corner square at the inside or the outside *(Figure 187)*? The inside option makes for a steep and fancy curve, and the outside is more of a simple arc. Mark the point you want on two sides of your paper corner square *(Figure 188)*. Mark a diagonal line between the marks as shown and sketch roughly the curve you want *(Figure 189)*. Once it looks about right to you, fold on the diagonal, darken in the final line, and cut the curve *(Figure 190)*. When you unfold the paper, you can then line up the two patterns to see how the corners will look *(Figure 191)*.

If your quilt is rectangular instead of square, do this exercise for the long side. There are several possibilities for the short side. The approach used by most quilters is to just unobtrusively lengthen or shorten a few units on the short side so that the corners match. Another possibility is to mark each corner and work toward the middle from both sides, letting the curves collide and form their own middle resolution *(Figure 192)*.

There! Now you have your own feathered vine pattern, custom-designed for your quilt. Just place the corner square in the corners and transfer the curve, then pin the long curve in place and transfer it all the way around. Double the line, if you want, by eye. Start anywhere you like and add the feathers in one direction all the way around the border *(Figure 193)*.

A shorter method for designing a curve is to measure the side and divide it into even units, then design just one unit *(Figure 194)*. Working with one section of the spine, it is a simple matter to lay it on the border, mark the end with a pin and move it along to the next place. This way you can see how it is going to work on

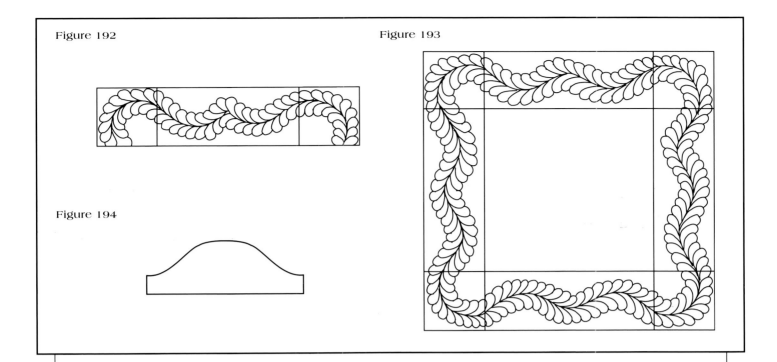

Figure 192

Figure 194

Figure 193

both sides and make adjustments if it is too long or short. Also, you can try starting at either the end or the middle of the unit at the midpoint of the border to see which way works best for the quilt.

This is all for those who want symmetrical vines. We sometimes just run the top and bottom vines from edge to edge of the quilt, then fill in the sides. You can just butt one side against the other, or you can put endings on them, as in *Figure 195*. If you want the vines to connect, as in *Figure 196*, the inner feathers need careful treatment. For us, it seems easiest to start in the corners and have all the feathers lean toward the middle of the vine. In the middle, just let the feathers meet and change direction. Here is the approach we used on a quilt called NINE PATCH (*Plate 37*, page 86).

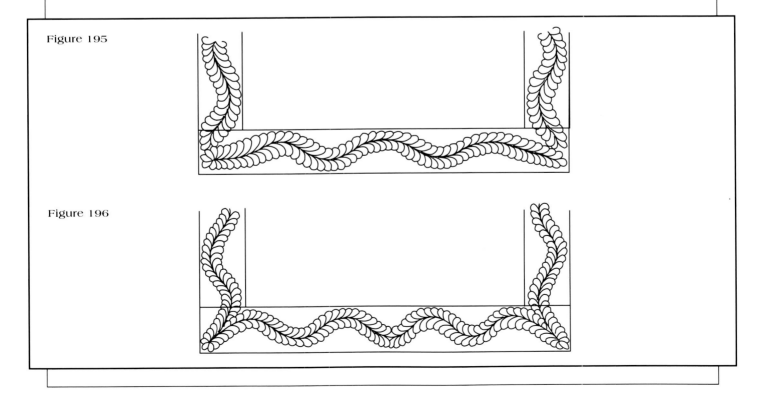

Figure 195

Figure 196

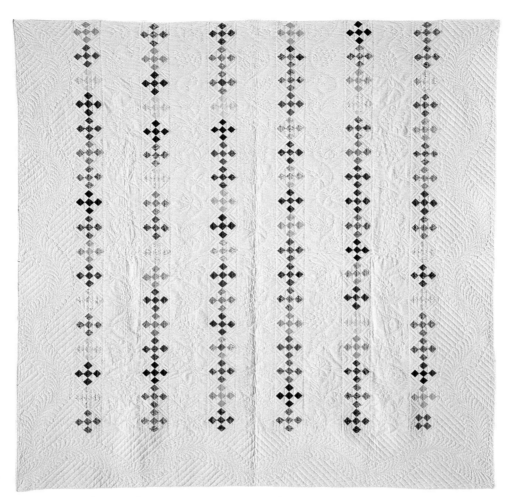

PLATE 37. Nine Patch, 80" x 84", 1986. Made by the Gwen Marston.
While this quilt was made with scraps given to us by other quilters, the quilt itself has a formal, elegant feeling. The quilting, Gwen decided, should be in the same vein. The plain bars make use of vines filled with a catalog of our favorite designs. The patterns are mirrored; that is, the outside bars are basically the same. Being drawn freehand, however, each one is slightly different from its twin. The feathers are thinner and taller than most, and the vines have endings, instead of turning the corners.

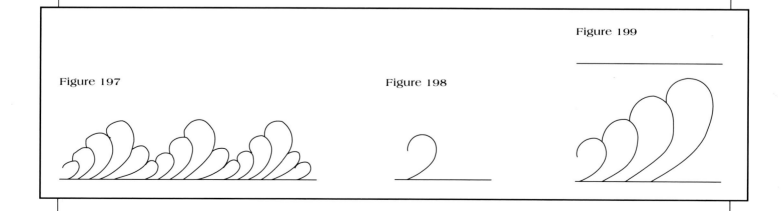

Figure 199

Figure 197

Figure 198

VARIATIONS

One of the most beautiful of all feather variations is one we call "the wave" *(Figure 197).* This seems to work best if you design one section and trace it over and over. A guideline is not necessary for the tops, just a straight line indicating the maximum height of the design. Start out with two lines 2½" apart. First, make one small feather, about an inch tall *(Figure 198).* Then make three more, each one taller yet *(Figure 199).* The fourth one should be the tallest. Make two more, shorter and shorter. That is all there is to it. The wave is a beautiful border design which looks even more rich with diagonal fill lines above it *(Figure 200).*

This approach, making the feathers taller and shorter, works for some dramatic feathered vine variations. The first one is best for fairly narrow borders,

about 3" to 4". Start with two straight guidelines 2½" apart, then put a freehand wavy spine in the middle, and double it like this *(Figure 201).* The spine should stay well away from the guidelines, and its curves should be shallow. Now add the feathers, drawing from the guidelines to the spine *(Figure 202).* Remember to keep them all the same width and to have the upper and lower feathers lean in the same direction. The shortest will be almost round, and the tallest will have long, curving tails. The success of the pattern depends primarily on the consistency of the widths of the feathers. Notice that these feathers break our rule of being perpendicular to the spine. Concentrate instead on letting the tails curve until they hit the spine, no matter where that curve takes you.

First cousin to the vine below is one

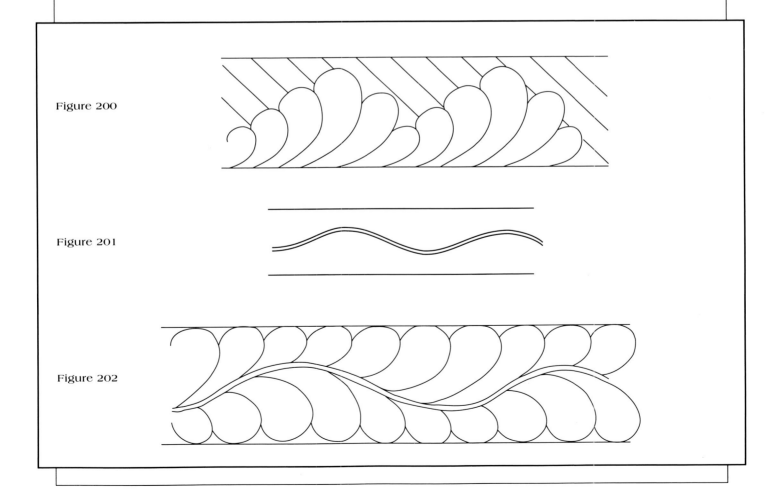

Figure 200

Figure 201

Figure 202

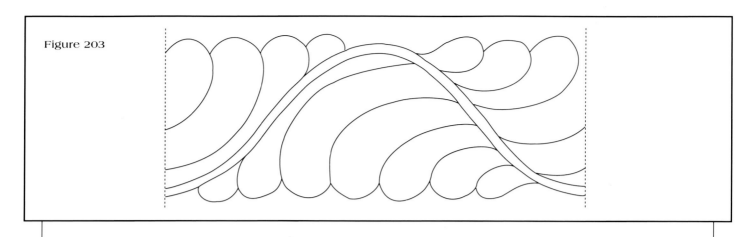

Figure 203

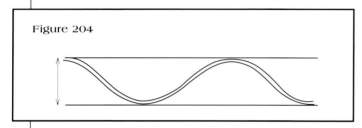

Figure 204

Figure 205

we have titled the "Finger Feather" *(Figure 203)*. Once again, start out with two straight guidelines, this time 4" apart. The spine, though, instead of being extra shallow, should be extra deep – it should reach all the way to the guidelines *(Figure 204)*. Unlike all the feather designs we have done so far, these feathers should lean in opposite directions. In other words, they should be just like the "incorrect" feathers in our example in *Figure 183*. Still, they need to remain a constant width. Remember to let the tallest feathers keep curving until they finally hit the spine.

We used this design on our copy of an Iowa Amish medallion quilt *(Plate 38)*. Notice the two corner treatments at opposite corners.

Not all feathers are run together in the usual way – some stand alone *(Figure 205)*. These individual feathers can be substituted for nearly all regular feathers to make new variations. The feathers are made of a simple loop. Draw these as you would regular feathers, with one penstroke. Start at the bottom of the leaf, then draw up, around and back to the starting point.

Feathered vines take on a new character with individual feathers. There is less quilting with these, but not much less. The main reason we use them is their open, unusual pattern. There can be considerable variation among the feathers with this kind of design, and part of the charm of the pattern is exactly this variation in shape.

PLATE 38. Variable Star Medallion, 82" x 88", 1981. Made by the authors.

We copied this quilt from the book, *A Gallery of Amish Quilts*, by Bishop and Safanda (p. 87). One reason we found the quilt so interesting was that each border had its own quilting pattern. At the time we made this quilt we decided, for some reason, we did not like the design on the purple border, so we used the finger feather. Other than that, we tried to copy existing designs like this. We learned a great deal about quilt marking. We tried plastic template making; we made paper templates; trying to keep the lines straight in the middle we invented our angle keeper; we rigged up a light table for tracing. Experiences like this have convinced us that the best way to understand old quilts is to make copies of them.

PLATE 39. Blue Tulip, 76" x 76", 1989. Made by Gwen Marston.
This is an original "folded paper" pattern, done in one of the old-time color schemes. Double diagonals seem to go behind the outline quilted appliqué. The outer border has a freehand seaweed feather. We wanted to include this quilt partly because it shows that sometimes we rush through the quilting and regret it later. We feel that we need to put it back in the frame and quilt in the empty spaces around the seaweed feather, where the quilt sags.

PLATE 40. Single Tulip, detail, 68" x 82", 1985. Made by the Authors.
Here is a section of a narrow border, about 3" wide, upon which we quilted the random feather. As you can probably tell, the design was drawn freehand.

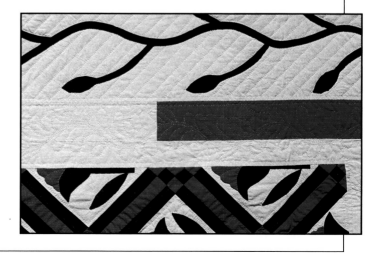

Figure 206

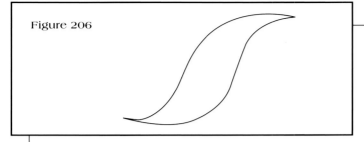

It may take a moment to get used to switching back and forth like this, but once you get used to the idea, you will find this pattern quick and easy to draft. We used this random feather on the narrow border of SINGLE TULIP *(Plate 40)*. Shown full size in *American Beauties*, page 35, plate 33. If you work with this design you will develop a personal version of it that will be unlike anyone else's, making it a great way to put your stamp on a quilt.

Another individual feather, though not strictly a feather shape, is the one we call the "seaweed" feather *(Plate 39)*. These can be much taller than most feathers, and can cover a wide border, up to 12" or 14". Draft them the same way as the individual feathers, but make the shape from two lazy "s" curves, as shown in *Figure 206*. The points should all face the same direction. The feathers are often fairly plump and almost birdlike in profile. These "leaves" vary in size and shape, and there is no exact repeat of the design, all of which results in a dramatic, energized pattern *(Figure 207)*.

Now we can try one of our favorite feather variations, the "random" feather *(Figure 208)*. As you can see, this design makes use of a number of the feathers we have covered – all at once. There is no "right" way to mark these, as the possibilities are numerous. Even the vine can be irregular and freestyle. We have used the random feather on borders as narrow as 1½" and as wide as 8". We simply draw a vine with no pattern, keeping it fairly shallow. Then we start with a few regular feathers, a few seaweed feathers, and an individual feather or two, and continue them as we like. Once again, this design has no exact repeat – it can change all the way around your quilt – so the result can be interesting and varied. Try it!

Figure 208

Figure 207

SWAGS

Some vines seem to be made of individual, swag-like units. These can be just a section of a feathered vine, with all the feathers running in one direction *(Figure 209)*.

Others are made as distinct units, with the feathers working outward from the middle *(Figure 210)*. These are beautiful and rich, and they are a breeze to draft and fit on a border.

Start out with the spine. Fold a piece of typing paper in half, then draw a line on it, as in *(Figure 211)*. Trace it onto the other side so your swag will be symmetrical. Start on the fold line with a pumpkin seed shape, top and bottom *(Figure 212)*. Then you can add feathers outward from the middle to the ends. On the very end, you can just stop, or you can put a "cap" on the space between the last two feathers.

We used a feathered swag on the SMITHSONIAN TULIP, shown in *American Beauties: Rose & Tulip Quilts*, page 36 *(Figure 213,* bottom). As you can see, we made the feathers a bit larger at the bend to make the design more square. The corner design is just a variation of the

Figure 210

Figure 209

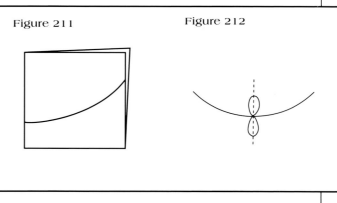

Figure 211   Figure 212

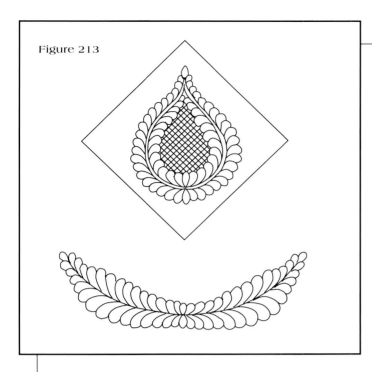

Figure 213

swag. For it, we started with a piece of paper the size of the corner square, then folded it diagonally. Once we sketched the basic shape we wanted, we darkened it in and traced it onto the other side for symmetry *(Figure 214)*. Starting with the pumpkin seed on the fold line, we just added feathers outward in both directions, then filled in the middle with crosshatching.

Below *(Figure 215)* are some other swag borders and corners. Study them to see how they were made.

These swags can be permutated infinitely. *(Figure 216)* shows a heavy one that reminds us of a handlebar mustache.

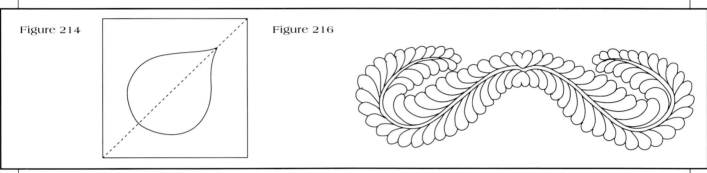

Figure 214

Figure 216

Figure 215

Figure 217

You can easily alter the length of a swag by opening or closing the curve upon which it is built. The one in (*Figure 217*) is more closed. It would work for a corner design, or even as a block filler.

When you look at old quilts with feather designs you will see that the rounded, plump feather with which we have been working is only one among many. Some feathers were much larger, some much smaller. Many are much thinner or fatter. We have enjoyed copying all kinds of feathers, and have learned that there is no single "right" or "best" shape. On Gwen's NINE PATCH (*Plate 37*, page 86), she wanted to use a tall, thin feather on the border. On FOUR PATCH MEDALLION (*Plate 41*) Gwen used feathers the same height, but about twice as wide.

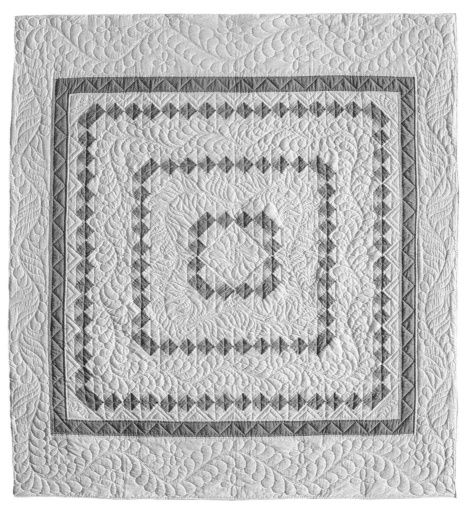

PLATE 41. Four Patch Medallion, 70" x 78", 1986. Made by Gwen Marston. Gwen made this quilt primarily as a vehicle for various feather quilting designs. Each border is different; each was drawn freehand. Notice the corner treatments and the small filler designs on the outer border.

Figure 218

PATCH, shown in Plate 36, page 86.

Other straight-line variations such as double diagonals, crosshatching, or hanging diamonds have also been used. Here is a feather with diagonal fill lines combined with fans around the inside of the border (*Figure 218*).

Another great way to fill these spaces is to use curved echo lines (*Figure 219*). Mary Schafer used these on ROSE WREATH, shown in Plate 19, page 26.

FILLERS

A feathered vine usually leaves rather large blank spaces between the curves. On old quilts these were nearly always filled with another quilting design, because the cotton batting had to be quilted closely to stay in place. Also, most quilters seem to have thought that a quilt did not look "right" until it was completely quilted down.

A simple way to do this is to fill the space around a feathered vine with diagonal lines, as we did on NINE

AMISH FEATHERS

Amish feathers are some of the most dramatic and beautiful of all quilting designs, especially Old Order quilting designs, such as those on quilts made in Lancaster County, Pennsylvania, before 1940 or so. While they seem at first glance to be complex, they are actually quite simple to draft. There are some continuous vine feathers like those we have already covered, but there are many more made of vines that start and stop. Two examples are shown in *Figure 220*.

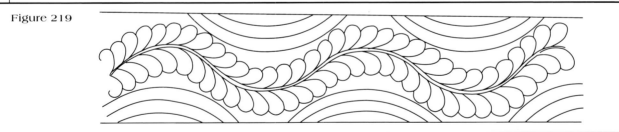

Figure 219

Figure 220

Figure 221

is all you need to design before you start marking the quilt. If you would like to try this, start out with a piece of paper this size, the width of your border and one-half its length. If you don't have an Amish quilt top for which to design, make your paper 12" by 36".

Now, fold the miter line of the corner and draw it in. This will show as the slanted, dotted line in our drawings. The vine we will design is like that in *Figure 223*, with a steep corner curve and a recurve toward the middle of the quilt. It contains the elements of many Amish vines.

Work lightly with a pencil to sketch

Notice how the corners of the vines have feathers going out in both directions. The feathers change direction against either a heart shape, or a pumpkin seed shape, as in *Figure 221*.

Most of these Amish feathered vines are symmetrical, based on a unit of one eighth of the border (*Figure 222*). So that

Figure 222

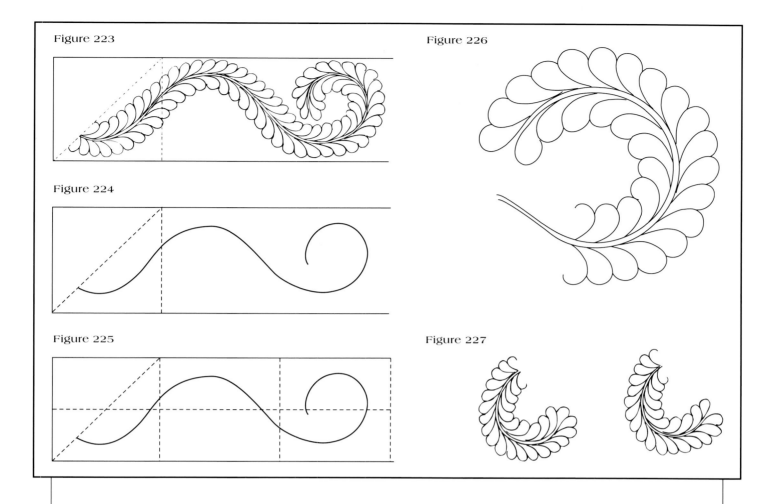

Figure 223

Figure 224

Figure 225

Figure 226

Figure 227

and scribble the first part of the curve, the corner. Start far enough up the miter to leave room for feathers on the outside of the spine. And get far enough from the miter to leave room for feathers on the inside of the spine. Do not try to mark the line with one pencil stroke. Just make many rough lines in the direction you want to go, and refine the line only when you begin to see where you actually want it (*Figure 224*).

At the top of the curve, stay far enough from the edge of the paper to leave room for feathers. Continue working on each part of the curve until you have a spine roughly like the one shown. If you have real difficulty, try marking a line down the middle of the paper and two vertical lines, as in *Figure 225*. Using these guides, check and see where each part of the curve crosses a line and reproduce that on your paper.

(You can use this "grid" idea when you are trying to copy any design.) Finally, darken in the spine line and double it.

Start on the miter with a feather on top of the vine. Then mark feathers all the way to the end, keeping the paper before you in one position. Most people find the most difficult point to be near the end, where the feathers follow the curve from "right side up" to "upside down" (*Figure 226*). Just relax and let the feathers follow the spine, concentrating on keeping them all the same height and width. And keep curving.

At the end, the Amish style of feather usually just stops. We sometimes put a cap on the end anyway (*Figure 227*). It depends on how accurate to the traditional designs you want to stay.

Unlike the spaces in other feathered vines, which are filled with diagonal lines or crosshatching, the spaces of these

Figure 228

Figure 229

Figure 230

vines are usually filled with more feathers. Most often, an arm extends from the vine and curves back through the empty space *(Figure 228)*. Sometimes the arm just "floats" *(Figure 229)*. But it can also be integrated, as in *Figure 230*.

It is rare, to say the least, to find two of these feather designs exactly alike. In *Figure 231* are a few more vines we have seen.

The open spaces are usually left unquilted, but sometimes are filled with small stars or pinwheels. When the quilts are rectangular instead of square, the space between the designs in the middle of the long side is sometimes filled with stars or tulips, sometimes with an extra feathered curve *(Figure 232)*.

We have our own way of marking these Amish-style feathers on a quilt top.

We start out with a paper pattern just as we did with the exercise above. We even go to the trouble of drawing the feathers so we can make sure the finished product is just what we want. Then we use the point of a compass to poke holes every inch or so along the spine. Once we have poked holes all the way along the spine, we can position the paper on the quilt top and use a pencil to make a dot through every hole. This gives us a "follow-the-dot" spine pattern on the quilt top. After we connect the dots to make the first spine line, we can double it freehand and mark all the feathers freehand directly on the cloth. Try this on a piece of fabric and compare it to marking in the slots of a template or marking around a small teardrop shape for each feather. For us, at least, freehand is the fastest and easiest way to mark them.

Figure 231

Figure 232

Figure 233

WREATHS

Perhaps the most popular feather design of all time is the feather wreath *(Figure 233)*. It comes in many flavors – large, small, double, single, and dozens more. Unlike some quilting designs, feather wreaths are found on nearly all types of American quilts.

Small feather wreaths, called "pinwheels," often fill small squares that are too large to be just criss-crossed, such as 3" to 6" squares *(Figure 234)*. Large feather wreaths almost always fill the Amish Center Diamonds. Of course, there are wreaths for all the sizes in between as well. And half or quarter wreaths can fill the triangles on the sides or corners of a top *(Figure 235)*.

The smallest wreaths are the easiest to draft to size. Start with a circle the size you want the finished design to be. Let's say you want a 4" design. Open your compass to two inches – the radius

of a 4" circle – and make a circle. Cut it out. Fold it in half, then in half again. Fold it once again and you should have a cone like the one in *Figure 236*.

Now you will need to trim the corners a little. Trim on the line indicated in *Figure 237*. The idea is to make the cone look

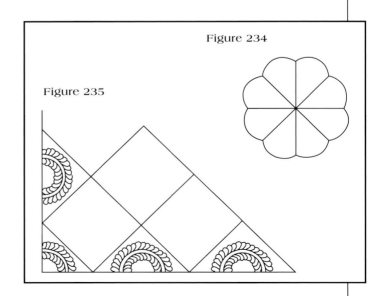

Figure 234

Figure 235

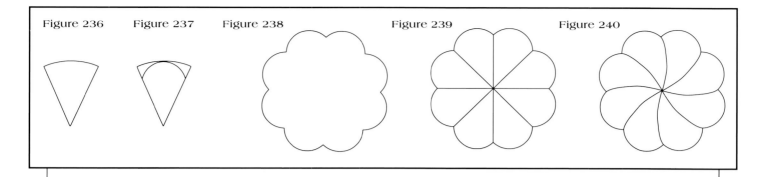

Figure 236   Figure 237   Figure 238   Figure 239   Figure 240

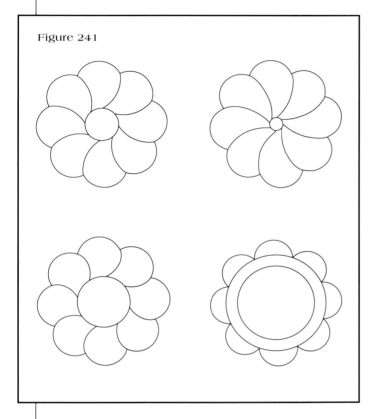

Figure 241

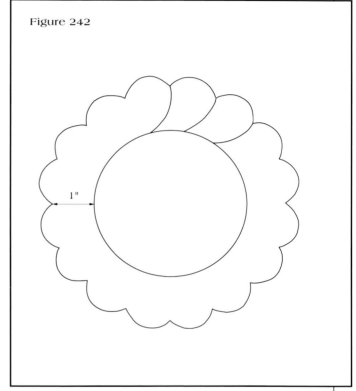

Figure 242

more or less like an ice cream cone. Trim and unfold. You should have a pinwheel like the one in *Figure 238*. On one side of the paper, just draw in the fold lines *(Figure 239)*. On the other side, draw arcs from the curves to the center *(Figure 240)*. Putting different size circles in the middle and drawing in the same arcs gives even more variations *(Figure 241)*.

Use the same system for wreaths up to 7" or 8", perhaps folding the cone once more before cutting, to make sixteen lobes instead of eight. For larger wreaths, the feathers are most often much shorter, like "normal" feathers. After you unfold the paper, use your compass to make a

circle 1" smaller than the valleys. Now, just draw the arc from the valley to the circle, as in *Figure 242*.

The interior of this design can be filled with anything you like, such as single or double lines, crosshatching, hanging diamonds, or pumpkin seeds.

It may have occurred to you that you could draw all the feathers on a wreath freehand. It's true. Folded paper works for certain sizes and shapes of feathers, but you might want to have more feathers than a cut-paper pattern will give you. There is no real secret to drawing these freehand feather wreaths, except that you should work with a pencil and make the

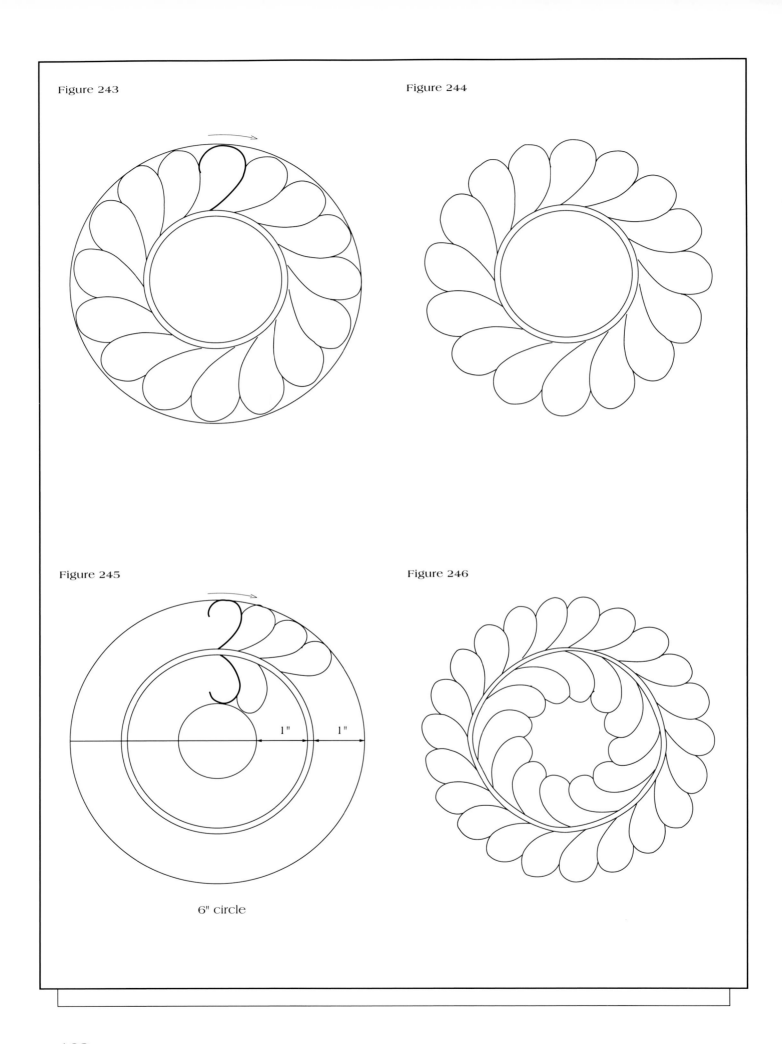

Figure 243

Figure 244

Figure 245

Figure 246

1"　1"

6" circle

first few feathers very light. That way you can erase and redraw them when you get back around the circle and find that there is not enough room for a full feather, or too much for one feather to fill.

You may find it easiest to have a guideline. Start with the feather on top, the darkened one in *Figure 243*, and work in the same direction as with all curves. When you get back to the first feather, you will probably have to erase two or three of the originals and make them a little thinner or wider to make the design work out as it does in the finished drawing *(Figure 244)*.

You can try this with feathers on the inside and out. Our example starts with a 6" outer guideline. There is a circle 1" inside that, another one which is ⅛" inch inside that, and an inner guideline 1" inside the inner spine *(Figure 245)*. Do not try to make the same number of feathers on the inside as the outside – there is not enough room. Just try to keep the inner feathers as wide as the outer ones and to let their tails curve more *(Figure 246)*.

It is not required that the inner feathers be the same size as the outer. In the next example you can see that the inner feathers are considerably smaller. Once again, there are no *rules*, only different ways of solving problems *(Figure 247)*.

To mark these feather wreaths on your quilt top, follow pretty much the same processes as you used to draw them on paper. For marking the folded paper wreaths on fabric, cut out the inner circle and transfer the pattern to cardboard *(Figure 248)*. Center the cardboard template on your block and draw around the inside and the outside. Then you can double the spine freehand and draw in the feathers.

For freehand wreaths, just cut a cardboard circle the size you want the spine. Center the circle on your block, draw and double it. If you want, you could use a chalk marker to make guidelines inside and out before you fill in the feathers. Remember to draw the first few feathers very, very light so they can be erased and redrawn if necessary.

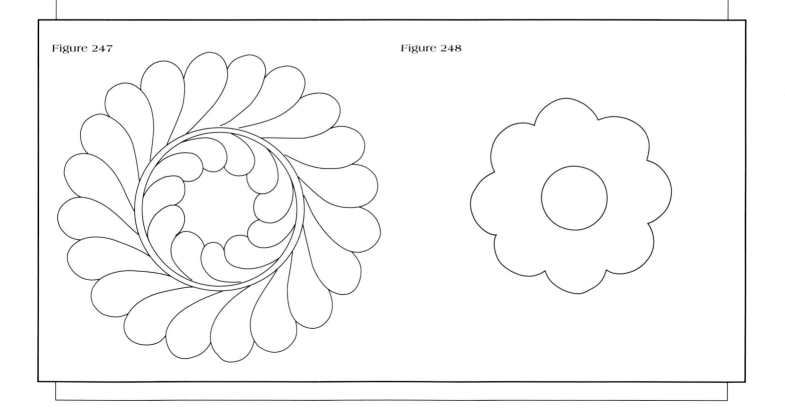

Figure 247

Figure 248

Figure 249

Figure 250

Figure 251

Figure 252

Figure 253

Figure 254

Figure 255

Figure 256

Figure 257

Figure 258

Figure 259

Figure 260

Figure 261

Figure 262

Figure 263

Using many of the concepts we have explored so far, you could endlessly invent new feather wreaths. Study the way the examples on these two pages were made (*Figure 249-264*). All of them can be drawn freehand, but *Figure 264* is much easier if the space for the feathers is divided evenly as shown in *Figure 265*.

BLOCK FILLERS

Collecting feather designs has been one of our hobbies over the years. We like the way quilters seem to have had fun playing with feathers, endlessly reinventing old designs and adding new ones to the tradition. It is perhaps in the feather designs made to fill blocks that the most customization has taken place. Quilters discovered that they could add feathers to virtually any shape and make it their own.

Amish quilts and old "linsey woolsey" quilts sometimes have a sort of feathered tendril, especially in large triangular areas. The design is usually made of three stems that meet at the bottom. Sometimes there are more than three stems, and sometimes you will see the stems gathered into a bow at the bottom.

Figure 264

Figure 265

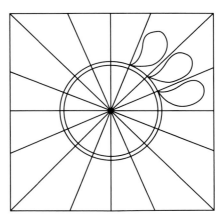

Figure 266

Figure 267

Figure 268

Figure 269

Figure 270

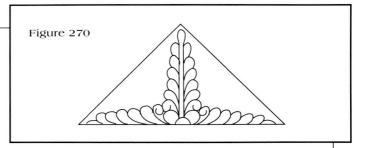

Figure 271

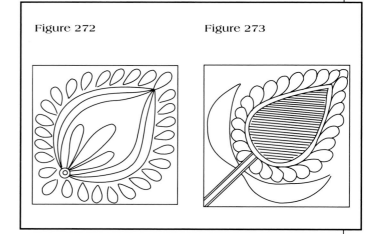

Figure 272   Figure 273

Figures 266-269 show some common treatments of the tendril.

Figure 270 could be used as it is for a triangular filler, or it could be doubled to fill a square.

Figure 271 is one of our own designs that starts out as a triangle and can become a square.

Another of our designs is a dubious "feather" candidate, but it does not fall readily into any other category (*Figure 272*).

One of the oldest quilts in our collection (IRISH CHAIN VARIATION, shown in *Sets and Borders*, p. 37) has a feathered pineapple that we have yet to use on one of our own quilts. It fills a block about 12" x 12" (*Figure 273*).

Figure 274

Figure 275

Figure 276

Figure 277

Figure 278

We saw the design in *Figure 274* on an old quilt in Kansas, filling a 24" square. When we first saw it, we were struck by its complexity. Drafting it, we were struck by its simplicity.

British quilts have some unusual feather designs, such as the "snail," a feathered spiral. To make it, start out with a freehand spiral and put the first feather on the open end; then work all around the edge as far as you want *(Figure 275)*.

A variation of this has a feathered tail that leads to a plain spiral *(Figure 276)*.

Two notable variations seen on British quilts are the "split" feather *(Figure 277)* and the spiral feather *(Figure 278)*. The split feather is just a fairly straight feather with a line in it. The spiral feather

Figure 279

Figure 280

Figure 281

Figure 282

Figure 283

Figure 284

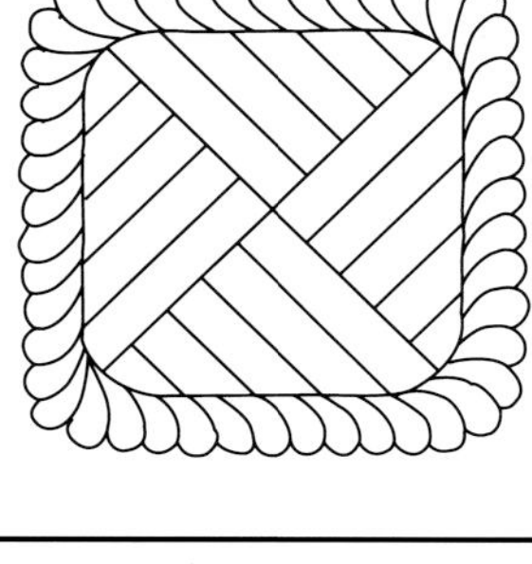

is usually seen as an occasional addition to a feathered vine.

One of the great unknown quiltmakers of this century was Betty Harriman of Bunceton, Missouri. From her collection of quilting designs we have selected a few feather variations that show some early design ideas *(Figures 279-284).*

Our friend Mary Schafer has invented a wide range of very individualized feather designs. One, shown in *Figure 285,* could be doubled to fill a square.

Figure 286, also by Mary, is a handsome design for those small triangles you sometimes wonder how to fill.

On page 109 are a couple of feathered hearts Mary designed for us. To make one of these, fold a piece of paper, draw half the heart, then trace the other half. Start with a pumpkin seed on the fold line and add feathers in both directions. The feathers can become larger toward the bottom, to enhance the "dripping" effect. These are filled with different crosshatchings *(Figures 287, 288).*

We took this idea and doubled the feathers for *Figure 289.* Notice also that these feathers start at the bottom and flow upward, meeting in the middle of the top.

Using only the ideas we have studied so far, you could mark entire quilt tops. *Figure 290* has the straight feather, the feathered vine, and feather wreaths.

Figure 285

Figure 286

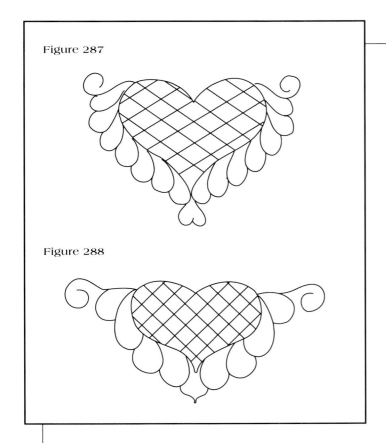

Figure 287

Figure 288

Figure 289

Figure 290

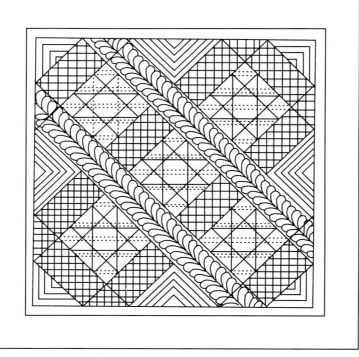

Figure 291

Figure 291 uses some of the straight line variations and a pair of straight feathers. All it needs is a border design. You can use your favorite one.

When you see any design you would like to copy or imitate, just break it down into the parts of which it is made. Is it mirrored? If so, you only need to design one half and then trace the other.

We want to repeat that we can only show a tiny number of quilting designs here. Our goal is to give you the skills you need to draft the rest.

Consider these patterns not as finished works, but as the bases for your own variations and inventions. By making small changes you can make any design your own. Once you start making changes you may find it hard to stop. Once you begin designing your own quilting patterns, you will find it much less enjoyable to try to fit someone else's on your quilts. Our closed swag from *Figure 217*, for example, could easily be changed with a couple of extra feathers and a few spirals (*Figure 292*). Now it looks almost British!

MARKING FEATHERS ON FABRIC

Once you feel comfortable drawing feather designs on paper, you can try marking one on fabric to see how it works. You can practice on a piece of dark fabric with a silver or white Berol Verithin® pencil and know that when you are done you can just wash the markings out.

Figure 292

Spread the fabric on a table top. We like a hard surface under the fabric for marking, but some quilters find it easier with a piece of cardboard under it, or a large cutting mat.

Let's start with a feathered vine. By now you should be able to mark these vines without the guidelines. Just transfer the curve and double it far enough from the edge of the fabric to leave room for the feathers. We like to pin the pattern to the fabric so it does not shift as we trace the vine.

You will notice that the pencil is easiest to handle if you hold it at an extreme angle, not straight up and down. What you want to avoid is dragging a lump of fabric in front of it. There will be a small bubble of fabric in front of the pencil, and you just have to learn how hard to press to minimize it. When you start marking the feathers, hold the fabric with your other hand, so it is taut and smooth where you are marking (Plate 42).

Remember to make each feather with one smooth motion, not a series of sketch lines. Also, learn to mark only as hard as you must to make the lightest line you will be able to see for quilting. Try to make each feather the same height, but do not worry about small fluctuations in size. These are part of your feather design's character and personality.

Fill in the feathers top and bottom, keeping them all the same height and width. As when you marked these on paper, the most difficult part will be the inside of the curves and the corner. Take your time and concentrate on keeping the feathers consistent. On the inside of the curve, remember to let the feathers have long, curvy tails.

Pinwheels will be easiest to mark if you make the template out of cardboard. Fold and cut your paper to make a small pinwheel, then trace it onto cardboard and cut it out. Poke a hole in the middle of it so you will be able to mark a dot in the middle of the pattern. Trace it onto your fabric and poke your pencil through the middle hole. Now you can follow the curves around from the outside edge to the dot, filling in the design (Plate 43).

You will soon see that it is easier to draw freehand than to trace around a template. The feathers will be easier to mark than the outline of the pattern. That is why we prefer to mark as much as we can freehand.

Continue trying all the feather designs you have learned. Work slowly and carefully at first, until you feel comfortable holding the fabric with one hand and drawing with the other. Spend a few hours one day becoming familiar with these feather-marking techniques and you will always be able to mark feathers on your own or anyone else's quilts.

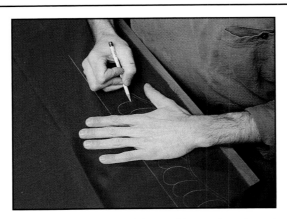

PLATE 42. Hold the fabric with one hand, and keep the pencil at a fairly steep angle.

PLATE 43. With cardboard templates, these small pinwheels are easy to mark.

CHAPTER 7

INDIVIDUAL DESIGNS

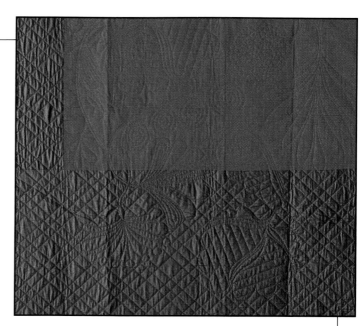

PLATE 44. Off Center Square, detail. Full quilt shown on page 147.

Quilting designs are as different and as individual as the quilters who make them. Many can be sorted into categories as in previous chapters, but many cannot. They range from the simple, such as basic floral shapes scattered freely across the quilt top, to the intricate, such as pictures of sailing ships.

On a tattered old quilt in our collection, the quilter used a small floral design to fill spaces left by the other quilting designs (*Figure 293*). We do not think it was marked on the top, but rather was freely quilted flower-by-flower, as the need to fill spaces arose. That is why all the flowers are slightly different in size and shape.

Quilters have used anything handy to mark their quilting designs: plates and saucers, thimbles, spools, cookie cutters,

scissors, even their own hands. For filling up odd spaces or plain blocks these techniques still work. We used cookie cutters for quilting templates on our ROSE OF SHARON quilt (*Plate 45*). We just drew around the horse and bunny shapes, then echo quilted inside them as necessary. The feather wreaths were drawn freehand.

Most block fillers, however, are more structured. Many of the 1930's Double Wedding Ring quilts we have seen have a propeller-like shape in the small oblongs. If you are thinking of how to quilt a Double Wedding Ring, this may be part of the answer (*Figure 294*).

Flowers have long been used as block fillers, particularly in bunches. *Plate 46* shows a typical design. Notice how the flower itself is derived from a

Figure 293

Figure 294

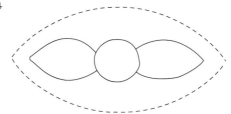

PLATE 45. Rose of Sharon, 36" x 36", 1987. Made by the authors.

PLATE 46. Detail. The Reel, (Variation), 82" x 86",
c.1875-1900. Maker unknown.
The quilting is stuffed on this damaged old red and
green quilt.

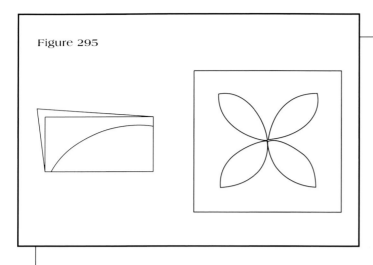

Figure 295

feather shape. You can design these and other floral designs using some of the same techniques we have worked with before.

A great shape to experiment with is the "pumpkin seed," another name for our familiar football shape. Fold a small piece of paper twice and cut a curve to make a pumpkin seed shape. For a small square, you can use four of these, as in *Figure 295*. Make a square of paper the size of your plain block, then fold it to make lines crosswise and diagonally. Align your pumpkin seed on the folds to make the next two designs *(Figures 296, 297)*. For a larger block, try making two stems on the diagonal lines and using the pumpkin seed to create the flowers in this design *(Figure 298)*.

Try the same techniques with hearts. Fold a piece of paper in half and cut half a heart as shown *(Figure 299)*. Use four of these to fill small squares *(Figure 300)*. For a heart wreath you can either make a circle and place the hearts as if they were going around the circle *(Figures 301, 302)*, or put the points inward, aligned with the fold lines *(Figure 303)*. Small hearts like this make dandy patterns for narrow borders. *Figures 304-309* present a few ideas to get you started.

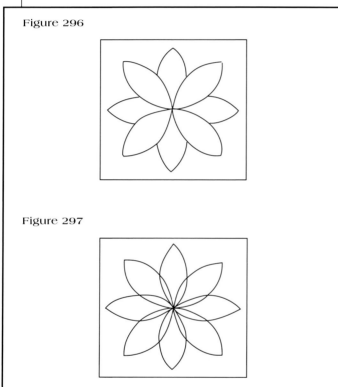

Figure 296

Figure 297

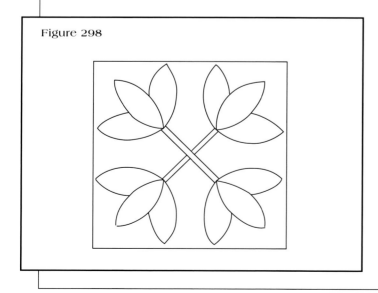

Figure 298

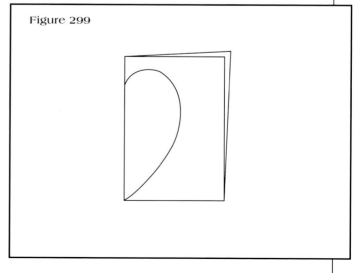

Figure 299

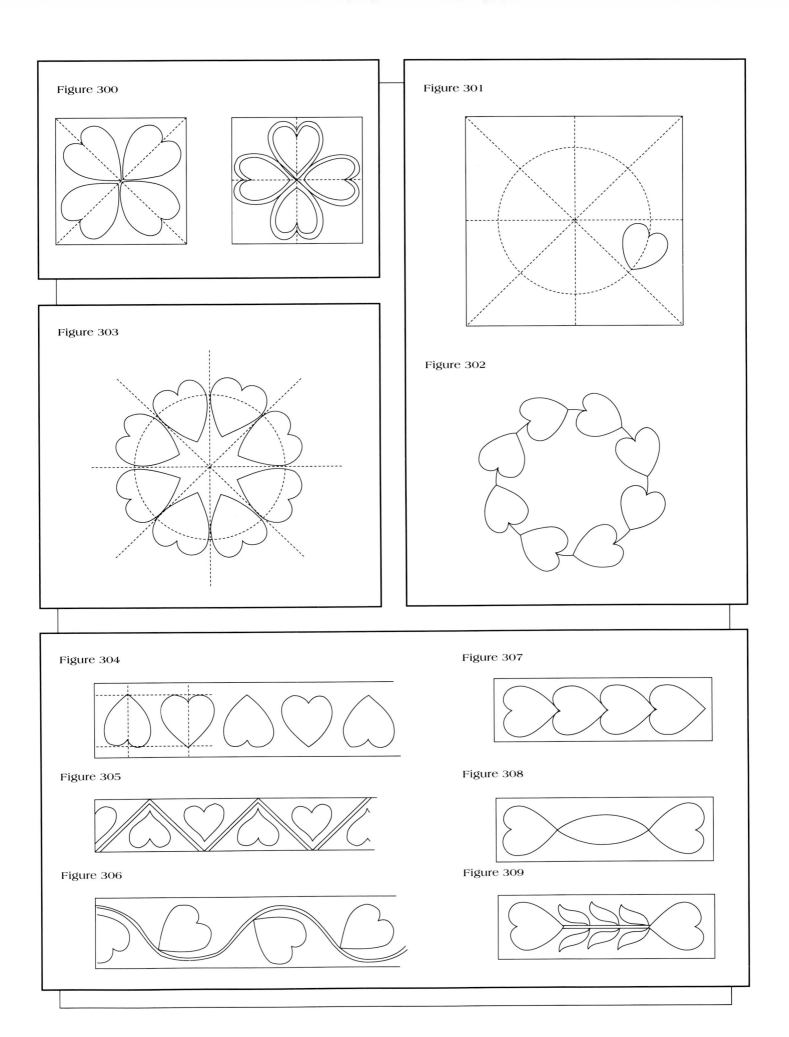

Figure 300

Figure 301

Figure 303

Figure 302

Figure 304

Figure 305

Figure 306

Figure 307

Figure 308

Figure 309

Figure 310 Figure 311 Figure 312 Figure 313

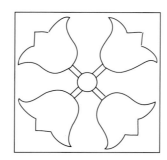
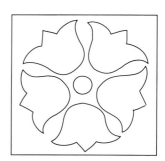

Tulips work, too. Some tulip variations of these ideas are shown in *Figures 310-313*. For the design shown in *Figure 313* we used a protractor to divide a circle into five 72° sections *(Figure 314)*.

As we have said, you do not have to be a designer to design a pattern. Try making some of these designs so you will see how simple they are. Then you will be able to better see how to make others.

Most of our students feel the same way about "drawing" as we do about preparing our taxes. They remind us clearly that they are not, they repeat, *not*

artists. Most of us are not trained artists, but all of us can learn to draw our own quilting designs.

If you have worked your way through the exercises thus far in this book, you already have drawing experience. You have been practicing drawing feathers, curves for spines and cables, and other shapes. You have also become more aware of the components and structure of designs. You know that drafting isn't as difficult as it seems initially and that it can be broken down into simple steps. You have ideas about how to draft symmetrical and asymmetrical designs. And you are more comfortable with the idea of drafting your own designs. All of this is good preparation for drawing designs for plain blocks.

We can break block filler designs into several main types: symmetrical and asymmetrical, floral (or pictorial) and abstract. We have already covered many of the possibilities in earlier chapters. Here we will work with some floral designs. Below are a few of our guiding ideas.

• Limit the number of shapes within one design. Most, but not all floral designs consist of a limited number of shapes. In other words, if there are three flowers, the flower shape is generally the same, even though the size may vary. If the design includes leaves, they will generally be similar in shape, though they may vary in size.

Figure 314

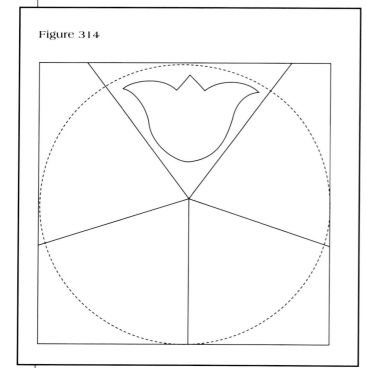

• Remember that you are going to quilt the design you are drafting. Therefore, keep the shapes large enough to quilt easily.

• Fill in the whole area as much as possible.

• Always begin by cutting a piece of paper the size of your finished block so that your design will fit exactly.

• If you want your block design to be symmetrical, remember that you only have to draft one section of the design, which can then be traced repeatedly to complete the whole design.

• If you are drawing an asymmetrical design, accept the fact that it will require experimentation. You won't sit down and draw the final design, but rather, you will go through several steps of changing and refining it.

To help you get started, we are giving you a dictionary of shapes, (pages 184-187). These are leaf, flower, and bud designs we have collected from old quilts, and some that we have drafted for our own use. We almost always refer to our dictionary of shapes to get ideas when we begin to draft a new design. We also have a folder of pressed leaves, an obvious source for ideas. As you become more interested in design, you will begin seeing ideas all around you. Floral shapes on fabrics, on wallpaper, from other types of needlework, on silver flat-ware and tea services, provide ideas you can use in your own design. Flowers from your garden are wonderful sources for ideas. Tulips and roses come in many shapes. Mums and zinnias go round and round. Bachelor buttons and old fash-ioned pinks are natural sources of inspira-tion.

You will notice that mother nature is always gracefully balanced, but never perfectly symmetrical. Leaves on the same branch are not identical in shape and placement. Flowers on the same stem are different sizes, and different shapes. Therefore, drawing floral designs freehand instead of tracing around templates results in more naturalistic designs. If, on the other hand, you want a more stylized, symmetrical design, tracing around templates will help you achieve your goal *(Figure 315)*. A free, asymmetrical approach to the quilting was used on the CHERRIES crib quilt *(Plate 47)*, page 118. All the designs were drawn freehand, with no patterns. The differences among the four main sections of the design are small. And, because a limited number of shapes were used, they all seem to make sense together.

SYMMETRICAL

Let's begin by drafting a simple symmetrical quilting design. *Figure 316*, page 119, is a quilting design we took from one of our quilts which was made by Joe's great grandmother, Minnie Roe.

What we want you to do is to try to copy this design. There are several advantages to it. Copying has long been central to the education of art students and is a sound method for learning how to draw. When you copy something, you become fully aware of the details in the composition. You notice how the line curves, where the veins in the leaf begin and end, how the end of the leaf may be slightly rounded instead of coming to a sharp point. The act of trying to copy

Figure 315

stylized   *naturalistic*

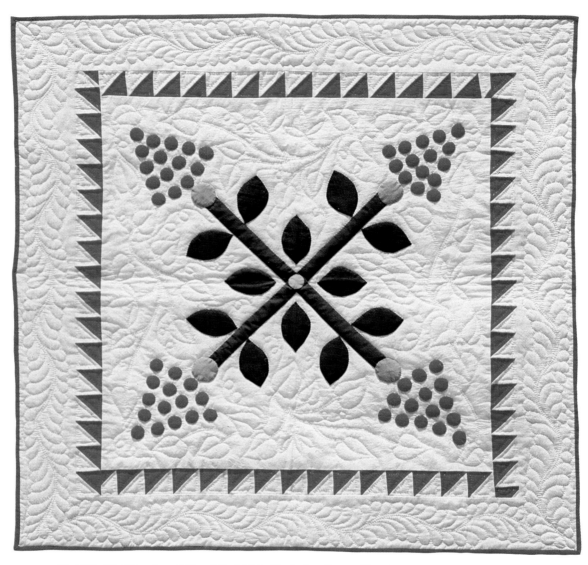

PLATE 47. Cherries, 34" x 34", 1991, Made by Gwen Marston.
The quilting on this original-design crib quilt was all drawn freehand. So, while the same shapes were used in all four quadrants of the block, all four were meant to be different. Notice the colliding corners of the outer feathered vine.

Figure 316

something greatly enhances your ability to "see." When we do this with a class of students the results are always excellent, and the designs are all somewhat different. Even when you try to copy, the resulting design will have your own special trademark. Follow our simple instructions to copy *Figure 316*:

• Cut a piece of paper 8" square. Fold it diagonally to create lines upon which you can center the shapes.

• On a separate piece of paper, sketch a tulip shape you like. Fold it in half and cut out the side you like best. Now you have a symmetrical template.

• Repeat this process for the leaf shape.

• Draw a circle in the middle of the 8" square of paper about the size we show in our design. Use a compass or a spool of thread. Don't measure the exact size of our circle, but try to gauge it by eye.

• Place the tulip on the fold lines. Check to make sure you have enough room for the leaf to fit in between the tulips. If you don't, trim down the tulip or the leaf slightly and try it again. Once you have your templates sized correctly, trace around all four tulips and then slip the leaf in between them and trace around it.

• Now study your design and compare it to ours. How is it different? If you are not pleased with your design, see if you can tell why and try the process again, making any adjustments you think will improve it.

Because we liked this design so well, we turned it into an appliqué block and used it on a sampler quilt. Later, we used the design in our drafting classes at one of our Beaver Island Quilt Retreats. Some of the women turned their designs into appliqué blocks and gave them to us for a friendship quilt *(Plate 48)*. We set the blocks together using ideas from our book *Sets and Borders*. When it came time to mark the quilt, we decided to draft slightly different tulip designs for all four

corners. It seemed like a logical idea since the blocks themselves are all varied. We used one tulip template to draft all four corner designs *(Figures 310- 313*, page 116). All four of these designs were drafted using the techniques described in our exercise.

ASYMMETRICAL

Let's move on and try some asymmetrical designs. For a preliminary exercise, try copying some of the flowers and leaves shown in our dictionary of shapes. Now choose a flower shape and a leaf shape that you like and feel confident about drawing. Gather together a pile of scrap paper, a pencil and an eraser, pour yourself a cup of coffee, and go to work. Perhaps donning an artist's beret would put you in the mood and make you feel more like an artist. The main point is to relax – remember that you are experimenting with something new and that you have a lot of scrap paper.

For this exercise you will make a design like that in *Figure 317*. Cut several

Figure 317

PLATE 48. Tulip Sampler, 59" x 70", 1990. Blocks made by friends;
assembled and quilted by the authors.

One challenge here was to set the blocks together in such a way as to have them make sense together. The strong red and white setting and border seemed to accomplish what we wanted. The quilting is mostly functional, with a few flourishes. There are four tulip quilting designs in the corners, and the word "Friends" is quilted into one of the lattice strips. The tulip designs are shown in Figures 310-313.

Figure 318

Figure 319

Figure 320

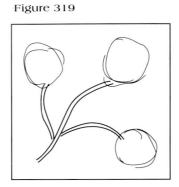

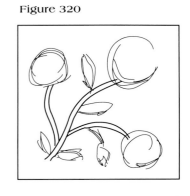

pieces of paper 10" square. Now block in the design. (By this we mean, roughly sketch the placements of the shapes lightly.) Sketch in the primary shapes, i.e., the flowers. Don't try to draw them as you want them to eventually look, but just sketch a rough circle to indicate where they will be and to help you determine what size they need to be *(Figure 318)*. Now sketch the central stem and the two offshoot stems *(Figure 319)*. The leaves can be sketched in next *(Figure 320)*. They are drawn in last because they can fill in the open spaces.

Now that you have the design blocked in lightly, begin to refine the design. Try to draw the flowers in as you want them to look. Make use of your eraser. Try cutting a shape from paper and using it as a pattern if you want to repeat it. Rarely will you get the design you want the very first time. Once you have all three flowers drawn as well as you can, refine the leaves. As you draw them in you may find that you need to move the flowers a little higher to make room for the leaves. This is all part of the process. You have to start somewhere and expect that it will take practice. We have drafted many original block fillers and every time we have to erase, refine, and often start over completely.

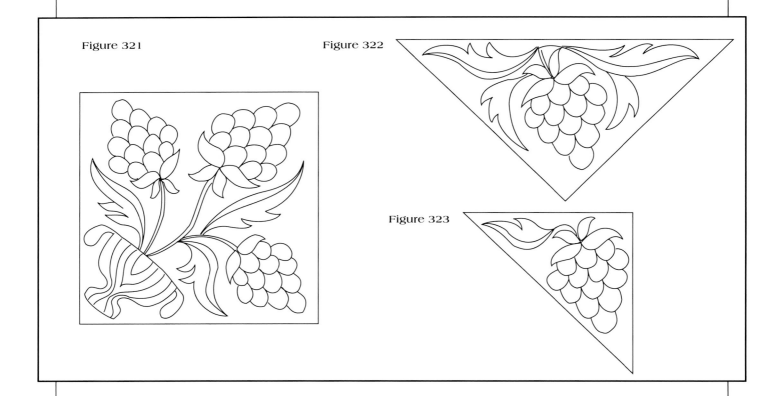

Figure 321

Figure 322

Figure 323

Select some other shapes and try the exercise again. Take a careful look at our examples for ideas. Use any technique you can think of to make the job easier. If you draw a flower shape you really like, trace it for the other flowers in your design. Try folding paper in half and cutting some tulip shapes that you can trace around. If you want to center the design or have guidelines at all, just fold the paper as we have done for other exercises.

TULIPS, HORSES AND WILLOW TREES (Plate 49), illustrates this technique in action on a real quilt. Gwen designed the quilting for the large plain blocks by going through the process we just described (Figure 321). With that done, she could just simplify it for the triangle filler on the sides (Figure 322). Even more simplification gave her the small design for the corner triangles (Figure 323).

PLATE 49. Gwen's Tulip with Willow Trees and Horses, 63" x 74", 1989. Made by Gwen Marston.

Gwen sometimes works on an appliqué project over a long period, in this case from 1987 to 1989. She was influenced here by the magnificent quilts of Susan McCord, which we saw in a long-running show at the Henry Ford Museum in Dearborn, Michigan. The borders have hanging diamonds behind the appliqué designs. The large white areas in the body of the quilt seemed to call for formal "fancy" quilting, so Gwen designed the basket of leaves and flowers for the squares, then made simplified, truncated versions of the design for the side and corner triangles. The designs are shown in Figures 321-323. The balance of the quilt is filled with hanging diamonds.

HIDDEN MESSAGES

We have talked about how quilting can enhance your work in many ways and how it can be a tool to make your work even more individual. It can also be used to make your work more personal. When Gwen made the HORSE QUILT *(Plate 51)* for her daughter, she quilted in hidden messages: a heart to signify a special love, a woman's symbol to celebrate their mutual pride in gender, and the date the quilt was made. These messages are particularly well hidden because they are quilted on printed fabric. The BUNNY QUILT Gwen made for her son Matthew contains hidden messages of endearment as well *(American Beauties: Rose and Tulip Quilts*, page 40). Unless you know where to look for them,

they are almost invisible. They don't detract from the overall design of the quilt, and they are a delight just waiting to be discovered.

As we were setting our TULIP SAMPLER quilt together (Plate 48), we couldn't help thinking of our friends who had so kindly given us the blocks. When we were marking it we drew the lattice design on by eye. On the last row we decided to quilt in the word "FRIENDS" in one of the lattice spaces. And we quilted a heart in the middle of the star next to it instead of criss-crossing the square as we had done in the rest of the quilt.

Quilting is also a good way to sign and date quilts. Our midwest Amish variable star quilt is signed and dated in the inner border *(Plate 50)*.

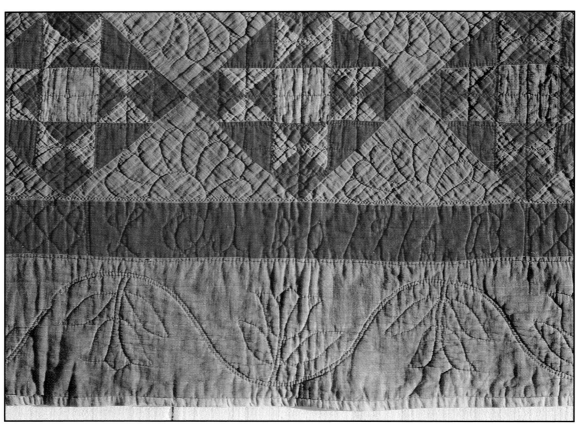

PLATE 50. Detail. Variable Star, 65" x 78", 1916. Signed "L.B." Maker unknown.

PLATE 51. Horse Quilt, 68" x 75", 1984, Made by Gwen Marston.
Collection of Brenda Marston.
The HORSE QUILT was made as a birthday present for Gwen's daughter, Brenda. The all-over fans are only interrupted by a few messages hidden here and there: a female symbol, a heart, the date, "love," and others.

CHAPTER 8

TOOLS AND MARKING

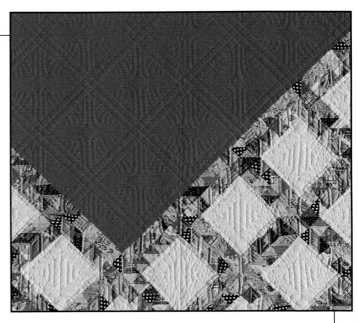

PLATE 52. Blocks, detail. Full quilt shown on page 139.

For at least the last two hundred years, there have been women who preferred not to mark their own tops. And there have been others who made a business of marking tops for them. We have known two church quilting groups, one Mennonite and one Methodist, that had designated "markers," women who marked all the tops that needed marking before they were put in the frame. The stories of eighteenth- and nineteenth-century quilt markers from Northumberland, England, such as George Gardiner, Joe "The Quilter" Hedley, and Elizabeth Sanderson, have been widely published. Writing in *Old Patchwork Quilts and the Women Who Made Them*, Ruth Finley describes a colonial American advertisement from 1747: "Sarah Hunt, dwelling in the House of James Nichols in School Street...stamped counterpins, curtains, linens and cottons for quilting" (p. 142).

Marking quilts is like any other discipline: the more you do it the better you become at it. Today there seem to be fewer markers than ever. It seems to us that the majority of quilters we meet find the marking of a quilt top the least enjoyable part of the quiltmaking

process. It is only natural that some would prefer one part of the process and some another. But we think there is more to the issue than that.

Aggravating the normal division of prejudices is the fact that little energy is spent on the marking process in most classes and books. This means that no one is really prepared for how difficult it can be to transfer designs to an entire quilt top. Right here, then, we want to let you know that marking a quilt top can be a tough job, and it may take you a few days of hard work.

You can imagine how much harder it was for our ancestors. Many had to work in cramped quarters, poorly lit, without many tools. Necessity, however, can be the mother of ingenious inventions. We have already mentioned how common it was to use plates and other kitchen items for marking. We talked to one quilter who told us that her mother had fan-quilted all her quilts, and that she marked the fans with her father's belt by anchoring the end of it and using the holes to hold the pencil to create successive arcs. Fans were also marked, we have been told, with knotted strings. With one end anchored and knots every ½", the marker could put a pencil through each knot and swing it in precise arcs.

Stores and itinerant peddlers sold all manner of tin and cardboard templates for quilting. Some templates had holes for "pouncing," or bouncing a bag of powder on them so loose powder would fall through the holes, leaving a "follow-the-dot" pattern on the quilt top. Simple shapes, such as small flowers, were to be drawn around. For cables and other designs, there were raised-edge tin templates that worked like cookie cutters. These were probably dusted with powder and pressed on the quilt top.

Quilters who wanted to have quilts without any sign of the markings, often scratched their designs with a needle. This method leaves a fugitive mark that must be quilted quickly, so scratching is done in the frame as one quilts. Scratching also had the benefit of eliminating the pre-marking process, so a quilt top could be put in the frame the moment it was finished. Thimbles and spools were handy for marking circles, usually scratched. Straight lines were sometimes "snapped" with a chalk line.

Chalk, pencils, and soap slivers were common tools for marking quilting lines, and perhaps cornstarch or flour for pouncing. Cinnamon, which has been cited as useful for pouncing, can stain.

Today there are modern marking tools that have been invented to make it easier to mark quilting designs on quilt tops. Some work very well indeed, and some seem to us to make life needlessly complicated.

We, like most quilters, tend to find tools we like and use them exclusively. Our attitude on this is the same as our attitude on all matters technical: we think you should find the tool that is right for you and use it. Here are some of our favorites.

THE LIGHT TABLE

One of the first phases in our quilt-making was our Amish phase. We made about twenty full-size Amish-style quilts between 1980 and 1982. We soon learned that the techniques and tools we had been using to mark on light fabrics did not work on dark ones. Wanting to trace many of our designs, we made a light table by removing a leaf from our dining room table, laying a piece of glass over the opening, and standing a lamp beneath the glass. Then we could tape the quilting pattern to the glass, lay the quilt top over it, and trace.

The arrangement worked, but it was far from ideal. In an effort to improve our system we tried brighter lights, dimmer lights, more and less room light, different pencils and markers, larger and smaller pieces of glass. The problem was always the same. In some spots we could see the pattern, but we could not see our marked line, so we could not tell if we were tracing closely enough, or if we were following our pattern at all. Also, we could not always see if we had marked a particular section until we turned off the light under the glass. If you have tried to rig up your own light table you are probably familiar with the problems.

At last we learned that the most important part of a light table was not the kind of glass or lamp we used. We learned that if we put enough thicknesses of paper on the glass, we would eventually reach the point where we could see *both* the pattern to be traced and our marked lines. Once we figured this out, using a light table became a pleasure instead of a chore.

You can make your own light table with materials you probably already have. All you need is a piece of glass and a light source to shine up through it. A brown grocery bag, opened up and taped to the glass, works well for dampening the light. We found an old beer sign from the bar on Beaver Island that was just an aluminum box, about 18" x 48", and about 3" deep, containing two long fluorescent bulbs. With a piece of glass on the top it makes a good, large surface for tracing.

Depending upon how elaborate you want to make it, a light table can take many forms. Even the simplest can be very useful. Just make sure to put extra layers of paper beneath your pattern so you can see both the pattern and your markings. Expensive light tables usually have a translucent plexiglass top to diffuse and attenuate the light. Plexiglass is not prohibitively expensive if you are going to use the light box quite a bit. If you rarely need a light table, you may want to use materials on hand.

When you use a light table, try to set it up so you can be comfortable working on it. For most patterns we find it easiest to tape the paper pattern to the glass, but for some it is easier to pin the pattern to the quilt top. If you have trouble keeping the pattern aligned one way, try the other.

PENCILS

Gwen's Mennonite quilt teachers instructed her to use a #4 hard lead pencil to mark her quilts. It makes a thin, light line that does not smear like softer lead pencils. The idea was to only mark lines dark enough for the design to be seen well enough to be quilted. A pencil line may not wash out completely, but it is so fine that the quilting makes it almost indiscernible. Gwen marked her first few quilts this way.

One of the first quilts we made together in 1979 had black bars and borders. A pencil, we learned, did not show up on dark fabric. So we visited an art supply store to see what other pencils or markers might be available. Our best candidate was one made by the Berol

Company, called "Verithin®." On its side was printed "Also ideal for marking blue prints." For a few moments we interpreted this to mean that it would work not only on red, green or brown printed fabric, but also on blue printed fabric. Of course, these are art pencils, and the manufacturer was simply pointing out that they could be used by designers or architects to mark on *blueprints*. We decided to try a white one for our quilt, and we bought a silver one to try on lighter fabrics. We also bought a few other art pencils, but the white and silver Verithins® continue to be our markers of choice.

We use the white pencil on dark prints and solids and the silver pencil on light prints and solids. Many quilt shops now carry Verithins® in white, silver, blue, yellow, and red. The red pencils are easy to see, but they were originally designed for making check marks and were made *not* to be erasable. We prefer to use only silver and white.

After much comparison and testing, we have found that the Verithin® has a very hard lead (making it hard to break), that it holds a point longer than softer pencils, and that it makes a thin, light line. The markings lighten considerably as your hand rubs over them while quilting, making them almost invisible by the time your quilt is finished. We are often asked if we wash our quilts when we are done quilting them, because the markings are so light they do not show at all. If we *do* have visible lines on a finished quilt, we can be confident that they will disappear with the first washing.

Since 1979 many other quilt marking tools have appeared on the market. Some have a chalk base, like dressmaker's pencils, and they come with thick and thin leads. There are chalk-filled devices in various shapes that make a thin chalk line. There are hard-edged tools for creasing, or "scratching" designs on fabric, as well as soapstone markers and graphite markers. There are also ink markers, the lines from which either wash out or vanish overnight. We recently visited our closest quilt store and bought one of each kind of marker.

Back at our Beaver Island "testing laboratories" we set out to compare the characteristics and performance of each. Here is the checklist we used:

• How does it feel in your hand, comfortable or cumbersome?

• What kind of mark does it make, light, dark, thin, thick?

• How easily does it erase or brush off?

• How long does it keep a point (where applicable)?

• How does it work for marking straight lines along a ruler?

• How does it work for freeform drawing?

• Does it do what its manufacturer claims?

• Does it perform the same on cotton fabric and others?

• What hazards does the manufacturer warn against?

We made a sample piece with two lines by each marker, machine quilted the lines, then washed the finished product. We highly recommend this sort of testing as the best way to find what works best for you. You might enjoy getting together with some of your quilting friends for an afternoon of your own testing.

Some of the chalk pencils were so soft they rubbed off too quickly, too easily. This could pose problems for hoop quilters, because just moving the hoop could remove the markings. This is not so serious with quilters who use the full-size frame, because the markings are not touched until they are quilted. Chalk-based pencils also tended to break more easily than others and to make wider lines. Some are much thicker than a regular pencil, making them feel awkward to us, especially for freehand drawing. The "rolling wheel" chalk markers made fine lines, but these lines came out too easily for us, and the devices were not comfortable to hold. They worked well for drawing straight lines, but we could not use them for freehand lines, such as feathers or floral designs. We even used thin slivers of soap for marking and had the same problems. The plastic "scratching" device, in addition to having the limitations of being applicable only for "mark as you quilt" situations, seemed no better than and not as handy as the quilting needle, which is already in your hand as you mark and quilt.

Ink markers designed to disappear with water or to vanish overnight have engendered controversy among quilters. We tried two: one designed to disappear when rinsed with clear water and one designed to vanish in 12 to 24 hours. Both resemble felt-tip pens and make a broad, dark mark. The packaging for both pens included instructions and warnings that are hardly reassuring. Here are some of the warnings.

• The pen should be tested on every fabric prior to use to make sure it will come out.

• The markings may disappear only to reappear, in which case special rewashing is required.

• Some soaps will set the markings and change them a permanent brown.

• Some fabric dyes may interact with the ink and set it.

• In some cases, ironing will set the marks permanently.

The instructions also were to mark lightly on the wrong side of the fabric, which is not practical for quilting. When we tried it we found that light pressure made the same dark ink line as heavy pressure, and that the ink bled through to the right side of the fabric anyway.

We have heard stories from quilters who carefully followed the instructions for an ink marker, only to have the markings reappear later, this time never to disappear again.

Still, we know experienced quilters who have used these markers for years and have had nary a problem. To us, the idea of testing all the fabrics in a scrap quilt to make sure the ink disappears is daunting. We tried a blue ink disappearing marker on one of our own quilts and were unable to remove the markings completely.

One of the marking pencils we tried, sent to us by Julie Hollowell of Bits and Pieces, a quilt shop in Dearborn, Michigan, is called "Karisma Graphite Aquarille®," by the Berol company. It is a graphite art pencil that is water-soluble. This pencil has been available on the European market for some time but was only recently introduced in the United States. The Aquarille® comes in very soft, soft, and medium hardnesses and was designed to be blendable on paper. We used a medium pencil on white fabric. It makes a wide, dark mark that does indeed wash out. We know a few quilters who say that as they grow older they need to mark quilting lines darker and darker so they can see them. The Aquarille® might be a good choice for anyone who has trouble seeing lighter lines.

In general, all the markers we tested performed as their manufacturers claimed they would. After all our testing, however, we have continued to use the Berol Verithin® silver and white pencils. Our second favorites are the chalk-based pencils designed for marking on fabric, which can easily be rubbed or washed out. No matter which marking implement you decide to use, make sure that you read and carefully follow the manufacturer's instructions.

ERASERS

Dressmaker's pencils are made with a brush on one end, on the assumption that you will mark some lines incorrectly and need to brush them off. No matter what marking tool you use or how well prepared you are, you need to be ready for erasing some lines. For our purposes, we like a white rubber eraser by the brand name of "Magic Rub®." These are widely available and work very well. For chalk or soap lines a soft toothbrush will do the trick. (Soap, of course, washes out.)

PAPER

Although we already mentioned butcher paper in our list of tools at the beginning of the book, it has become such an essential part of our quiltmaking that we wanted to mention it again. We are referring to the plain white wrapping paper butchers use, not the waxy freezer paper they sometimes wrap messy items in. Living as we do on a remote island with a small friendly grocery store, we know the butcher well enough to ask him to order rolls of paper for us; we have no idea whether you can persuade butchers on the mainland to do the same.

If you *can* find a friendly butcher who will order you a roll, you will probably be inclined, as we are, to treat him or her very well. We use the stuff when we want to work out large sections of pieced or appliquéd quilts, when we want to design a full-size quilting pattern for a long border, when we need to design a large block...in short, whenever we need paper larger than typing paper-size.

We also get the butcher paper and crayons out when we have company with children.

Our friends and family are used to receiving presents wrapped in either plain white paper or plain white paper decorated by the above-mentioned children.

We have also used it for dress patterns. Being teachers, we have gone through many rolls by taking them to class and cutting off lengths for quilters to use in class or to take home.

RULERS

Our favorite rulers are made by the Omnigrid™ company. They are clear and have absolutely accurate markings printed in black and yellow so they are visible on all fabrics. We have a complete set of these rulers, from the small 1" x 6" model to the big 15" square one. We have used them for years, and they show no sign yet of wear.

We use these for our rotary cutting guides, for pattern drafting, and for drafting and marking designs for quilting. Joe uses them when he wants to design a bookcase. Gwen used them in drafting all the designs for this book.

There are, of course, many rulers on the market which are made for quilters. Most of them will work fine for drafting quilting designs and pattern drafting. We suggest you try a number of brands before you choose one.

TEMPLATE MATERIAL

For making templates we almost always use cardboard. When Joe is lucky enough to have some of his shirts professionally laundered, he always has them folded, rather than hung. That way we get a nice piece of cardboard with each one.

If you do not want to cut the backs from your legal pads, as we do, or cut up cereal boxes, as our friend Mary Schafer does, you can buy posterboard at most grocery stores.

We have sometimes used plastic template material for our quilting design templates, but have found that we prefer cardboard. For one thing, we rarely use the same template twice, and marking a single quilt does not seem to wear out a cardboard template. For another, we like the idea of recycling cardboard found at home!

When we do use plastic, we like the sheets that have a non-slip finish on the back, found at quilting stores. We have used X-ray film, coffee can lids, and even, on occasions, milk jugs.

Aside from these marking tools, we use the same tools we indicated at the front of the book: protractors, compasses, felt-tip pens for darkening patterns to be traced, etc. We mark our quilts for quilting in the full-size frame, but few others use a frame, and there are differences in the way you mark for a frame or a hoop.

MARKING FOR THE FRAME OR HOOP

We quilt in an old-fashioned, full-size frame, the kind in which the quilt is stretched tightly and held by four long boards. With this type of frame, and this type only, the quilting is done from the outside in. One advantage of the frame is that the markings are not rubbed or smudged as you work. Therefore, we can mark the entire quilt top before we begin quilting with no fear of the markings fading with wear.

The story is different with a hoop. Markings receive a lot of brushing and rubbing as the hoop is moved around, not to mention brushing against furniture and clothing. Some of the easily erasable lines from chalk markers can be gone in moments. Once again, we like the Verithin® pencil, or a similar hard marker, for hoop quilting. Remember that even these markings will eventually brush off, however, so they may need to be redrawn if a quilt is in the hoop for a long time. The trick is to watch for this, so they can be touched up before they disappear altogether.

This tendency for markings to brush off during hoop quilting is probably one reason for the popularity of disappearing-ink markers. They will stay brightly visible no matter how much a quilt is brushed or dragged around. Because of the risks associated with them, however, we prefer to recommend a more assuredly removable marker, such as the Graphite Aquarille® mentioned previously. Its dark marks will come out with a normal washing.

With some designs it is possible to mark as you quilt. It is more difficult to place designs accurately, and often harder to draw them on a soft layer of batting and backing. We find it easiest to place a thick book or bread board under the hoop to provide a firm drawing surface. Some designs, however, do not lend themselves to this technique. Long diagonals are hard to mark in sections. And any designs that need a light table for tracing are not suitable for "mark as you go."

Our friend Sally Goodin, a proficient and adventurous quilter and quilt teacher from Columbus, Indiana, invented a way to quilt all-over fans in a hoop, marking as she went. Instead of the usual method of quilting from the inside of a quilt outward, she quilted fans from the outside towards the center. She marked and quilted the largest arc of one unit, then quilted the rest downward in freehand ½" increments. Then she moved the hoop, marked another large fan and filled it in. She continued to build row upon row of fans around and around from right to left. Sally's Star quilt is perfectly executed (Plate 54).

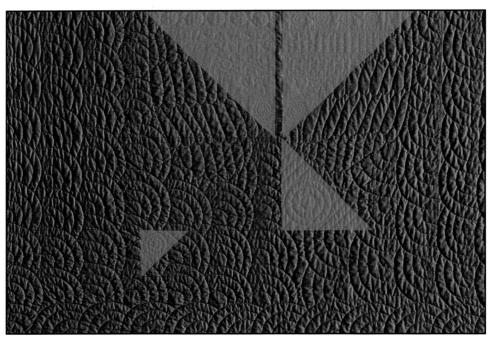

PLATE 53. Detail, Dancer, 72" x 80", 1985. Made by the authors. Full quilt shown on page 143.

PLATE 54. Chris's Lone Star and Stripes, 82" x 96", 1988. Made by Sally Goodin.
This powerful quilt was made by one of our favorite quiltmakers, Sally Goodin, of
Columbus, Indiana. Notice that the fans are quilted right across the pieced design.

MARKING REVIEW

Here is a review of the ways we think it is easiest to mark the major quilting designs.

STRAIGHT LINES

First, make sure that you *need* to mark the straight lines. Many fine old quilts have diagonals or perpendiculars quilted freehand. The natural variation in angle and straightness of the lines gives an effect like no other. We never mark outline quilting or criss-cross lines in squares. If you are incurably worried about these you can always scratch the lines in as you go.

For short straight-line designs – the ones on blocks and borders – we use our angle-keepers and rulers. If the lines are perpendicular we just make a perpendicular angle-keeper. On narrow Amish borders, for instance, we use a small right-angle template (*Figure 9*, page 27).

Another handy tool is a carpenter's square. We use one often for keeping lines truly square and accurately measured.

Long lines that cover all or a large part of a quilt top are difficult to keep aligned. Look at this kind of quilting on old or new quilts and see for yourself how few have been able to keep their lines and angles accurate. The solution is to use angle keepers and a long board. See *Figures 17-21*, page 29 for details.

CIRCLES

Small circles, freely placed, can be scratched around thimbles or spools as you quilt. Some designs do need to be marked ahead of time, but do not need to be exactly duplicated with each repetition on the top. For grape bunches, for instance, we sometimes mark them freehand on the top, using a dime or a nickel for a template. That way, each bunch of grapes looks essentially the same, because all the grapes are the same size, but each bunch is slightly different from the one before.

For most clamshell and teacup designs we use a cardboard circle with crosshairs on it. Sometimes you may want to use this circle to mark the pattern on a piece of paper exactly the size of the part of the quilt it will fill and trace it on. Use a light table if you cannot otherwise see to trace.

FANS

If you quilt in a full-size frame, consider quilting all-over fans freehand. It seems frightening at first, but everyone we know who has tried it has found freehand fan quilting to be liberating and exciting.

Even if you choose to mark fans, consider quilting double or triple ones freehand. That is, mark the original fan, then quilt the second and/or third one freehand. You will soon see that you cannot wander too far from where you want to be, as you always have a guideline close by.

If you want to quilt all-over fans with a group of quilters at a frame, make a cardboard template of the largest one, as in *Figure 87*, page 53, and mark the large arcs so everyone can start at once. Have them fill in the smaller ones freehand, perhaps a needle-length apart.

For almost all marked fans, we prefer to mark one or two units on a piece of paper and trace.

CABLES

Cables have long been marked with templates, usually with slots for the long lines. For us, however, it is easiest to trace cables. This means drawing the pattern on paper first. We like to use a piece of paper either the length of the border or one-half the length of the border and to pin the paper in place under the border. That way we can work out the corner or middle resolution just the way we want it before we start marking.

FEATHERS

As we have said, we usually mark feathers freehand on the quilt top. Sometimes we even draw the spine freehand, especially if we want an informal, free style. For large Amish-style feathered vines, we draw the spine on paper and punch holes in it every couple of inches. Then we can pin it in place on the top, poke our pencil through the holes, and connect the resulting dots. For most continuous vines we just fold and cut paper to make the curve. Either way, once we have one line of the spine drawn, we double it freehand. If you try this, just remember to take your time. If you wander too far from the original line, you can either erase the mistake or just stay closer to it when you quilt.

Feather designs that are not vine shaped, that is, feathered hearts, feathered spirals and the like, can be drawn freehand or they can be traced, depending on the degree of formality you want.

Feather wreaths come in great variety. Large, Amish-style wreaths we treat much like vines: once we have the circular spine traced on and doubled, we just draw the feathers freehand. Mark the first one very lightly, so you can erase and redraw it fatter or slimmer as you need when you get all the way around.

Smaller feather wreaths are easiest for us to draw with a template, like the one shown in *Figure 248*, page 103. The inside can be filled with feathers, straight lines, or the design of your choice.

INDIVIDUAL DESIGNS (BLOCK FILLERS)

Many block fillers are best traced. Often, however, we end up using a combination of techniques, such as an angle keeper for some diagonal fill lines, a circle for the clamshell, and a freehand flower.

We have also developed a taste for drawing block fillers freehand. If you can draw a shape on paper you will probably be able to draw it on fabric. You can always experiment on a piece of fabric that needs to be washed.

CHAPTER 9

FINAL WORDS

PLATE 55. Rose of Sharon, detail. Full quilt shown on page 113.

The first time we made a large quilt and put it in the frame, it looked like an ocean of fabric. We wondered if we would ever get it done. We did get it done, eventually. Along the way we had a lot of fun and learned that it does not really take patience to make a quilt – it takes a certain amount of impatience. When you want badly enough to see something finished you will enjoy every bit of progress and get a thrill every time you roll up a finished section.

Also, we truly think that the more time and energy we expend on a quilt, the more we appreciate it, up to a point. We have found that, for us, it is simply very important to quilt thoroughly. Some of our rushed pieces that we most wanted to get done and out of the frame, look that way to us – rushed, incomplete. After a few quilts you will have a better feeling for what you like, for the kind and amount of quilting your quilts need. There is really no way to know what you like in quilts other than to try it and see.

There is a lot to learn about designing your own quilting designs. If you look at it like work, you will probably get bored and quit long before you have learned much. The only way it will all make sense is if you work on these ideas one at a time in the context of making your quilts. That is, the next time you have a finished top that needs to be marked for quilting, look at some of the examples in this book, and, of course, look at pictures of old quilts and imagine that you could draft any quilting design you see. If you cannot find the instructions for what you need here, figure out some way to do it. That's right. Just believe that you can figure out some way to make these designs that would be as good as anyone else's.

In the end, that is what we are after. Using the ideas in this book – folding paper for symmetry, using guidelines, accepting slight variations in shapes, building complex designs from repeated simple shapes, etc. – you should be able to improvise on your own. Remember that there were no classes, no books, no teachers in the last century. Women just made it up as they went along. And if they could, you can.

Try to have a long view of quilt-making. What seems endless today, such as a quilt that takes three months of work, will be around for a long time. Ten years from now, that three months will not seem like so much. And remember too that part of the fun of making quilts over the long haul is how they change and mature. We tend to feel that we should be making masterpieces from the beginning. That is impossible. The definition of a masterpiece is that it is made by a master. No matter how much you learn and do, it will take years before you are a master at your craft. So do not worry about making a masterpiece, and do not worry about making a minor piece either. Just try making the quilts that appeal to you the most and see how you feel about them in a decade or so. Your tastes and your eye will change. But there is no other way to learn everything you want to learn than by doing it.

When Joe went to college, he studied English, literature, and creative writing. He learned a lot. But, when he tried to start writing articles and books, he learned a lot more. The knowledge you get out of this or any book is like that. It only sinks so deep. It is when you put it to work that you really "learn" it.

Of course, then, you cannot learn everything at once. With quilting designs you can just work on them as you need them. Remember that the quilters you admire and respect went through the same process you are going through. They learned one thing at a time and put it to work in their quilts.

Working on quilts or any creative process can be lonely. For us it helps to remember that we are not alone. We are not the only ones who have ever felt intimidated, who have ever felt inadequate to the task, who have ever wondered why we started this in the first place, or who have ever gotten halfway through a quilt and had a sinking feeling that there was something wrong with it.

These feelings are all part of the creative process. Try not to worry about them. Just keep working and you will soon feel some of the other feelings that are part of it as well: the feeling that you *are* the only one who ever made this particular quilt, or that, unlike with many of your daily activities, here you have something to show for your efforts. And nothing can top the feeling of getting a quilt done and sharing it with those you love.

GALLERY OF QUILTS

PLATE 56. Gwen's Tulip with Willow Trees and Horses, detail, full quilt shown on page 123.

The quilts shown here are meant to give you an idea of how we have put our theories and techniques into practice. They are in alphabetical order, not chronological order, and not grouped into various styles. To us, a quilt is a quilt, and we like one kind as well as the next.

Some of these are from a series of quilts we made in the mid-1980's, when we were exploring the idea of simple piecing and fancy quilting. We got the idea from our studies of old Amish quilts and early "linsey woolsey," or, more properly, "glazed wool" quilts. It seemed to us that, while many other aspects of the quilt tradition were being explored and extended, these kinds of quilts were being ignored. On our "minimal" quilts we sought to use unusual, sometimes extravagant patterns that we had not seen used much in modern times. We decided to overlay them on simple, rich fields of color, assembled for just this purpose. It appealed to us greatly to make a bold statement of color that could be embellished with lyrical quilting. Also, it appealed to us to turn the tables on modern quilting, and make quilts that *had* to be richly quilted for their artistic survival.

Some of the quilts shown here are more conventional, such as the Amish BARS quilt, or the untitled blue and pink strippy quilt. On these quilts we have tried to keep the quilting stylistically consistent with the piecing.

A few of these quilts are antiques we have found it helpful to study. From some of those we have taken patterns, from others only inspiration.

All the quilts are made of cotton fabric, machine pieced or hand appliquéd; all but WHIG ROSE are hand quilted. All of these quilts are in our collection unless otherwise noted.

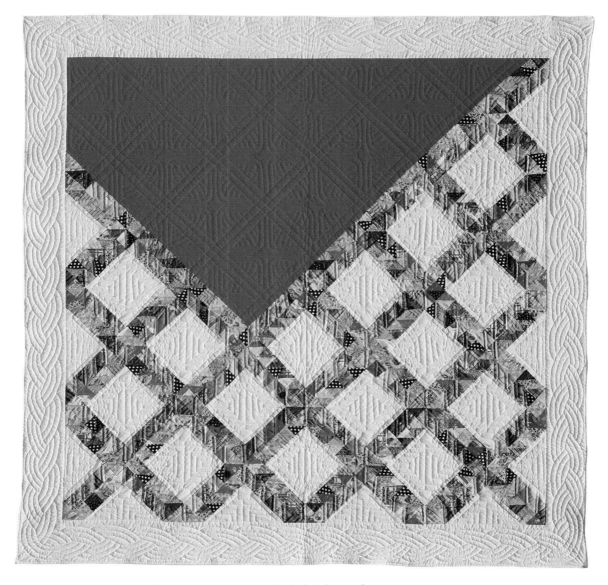

PLATE 58. Blocks, 76" x 76", 1990. Made by the authors.

This is one of a series of quilts on the theme of homelessness. The title and the design refer to both the streets where homeless people live and the obstacles to self-improvement. This quilt seemed to call for formal, tightly controlled quilting. The outer border has a braided cable from a Roman vase, and the inner designs are mostly geometric. The geometric designs were worked out by experimenting with an angle keeper.

PLATE 57. Nine Patch, 70" x 70". Pieced by the authors, 1989, quilted by the authors, 1992.

Gwen drafted the all-original quilting designs on this quilt. Our idea was to use a different design in every block of this simple quilt to demonstrate how fancy quilting can transform a humble quilt top. Twelve of the designs are shown in the pattern section. The outer, "dogtooth" border was cut freehand from folded fabric, to give it a looser, less regular feeling than a pieced sawtooth border would have.

PLATE 59. Bull, 72" x 80", 1984. Made by the authors.
We have long been interested in folk art of all cultures. This quilt was influenced by our small collection of Central American folk textiles. Except for the straight lines marked with an angle keeper, the quilting designs are mostly original and were all drawn free-hand. They were influenced by our studies of quilts from the British Isles. Making an original quilt, we feel free to use quilting designs any way we can conceive.

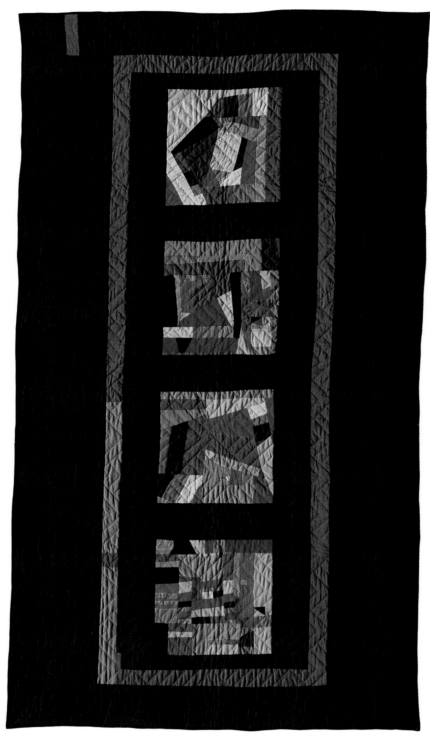

PLATE 60. Crazy Quilt, 44" x 79", 1987. Made by the authors.
Private Collection
This size of quilt is often called "hired hand," so-called because quilts were
sometimes made for the narrow beds upon which hired hands slept. Gwen
pieced the top and Joe designed the quilting. The quilting designs vary,
from geometric and organized, to organic and freely drawn. Joe's chief
concern was doing something that would do justice to one of Gwen's best
quilt tops.

PLATE 61. Dancer, 72" x 80", 1985. Made by the authors.
Collection of Valerie Clarke.
We made this quilt in exchange for a large photographic work by our friend Valerie
Clarke. The main idea for this kind of design is the early "linsey woolsey" or "glazed
wool" quilts, which often have large expanses of richly colored fabric, densely quilted.
The quilting is mostly derived from aboriginal rock inscriptions, and was mostly drawn
freehand.

PLATE 62. Garden Island, 76" x 87", 1984. Made by the authors.
Collection of Don Dwyer.

While this quilt borrows some ideas from Amish and glazed wool quilts – in its large expanses of plain cloth heavily quilted – it is one of the few we have made that are wholly original inventions. The quilting designs were inspired by the lush vegetation on a nearby island.

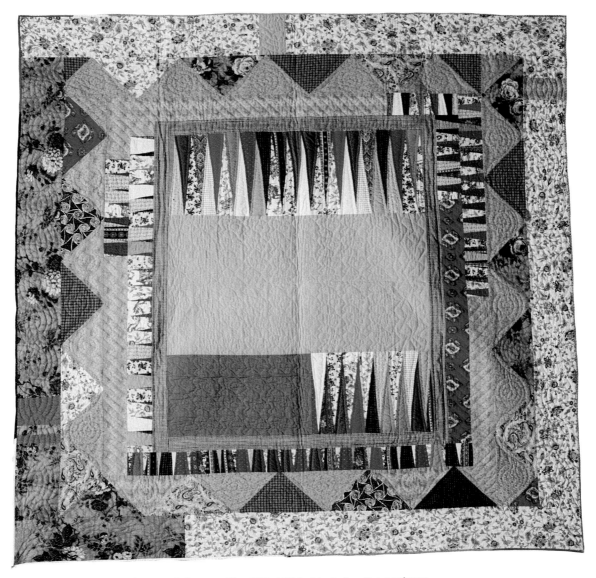

PLATE 63. The Martinique, 70" x 70", 1989. Made by the authors.

Like BLOCKS (page 140), this is a quilt that we were motivated to make because of our concern for the plight of America's homeless citizens. It was named for a notorious, and now demolished, "welfare hotel" in New York, where homeless people were housed in substandard conditions at great government expense. Our idea was to portray a space surrounded by chaos and broken things. In the center field are quilted repetitions of a seated figure taken from an ancient rock inscription. The more traditional quilting on the borders is either outline quilting, as on the long points, or cable variations, as on the two outer borders. All corners were "chopped," in keeping with the pieced design.

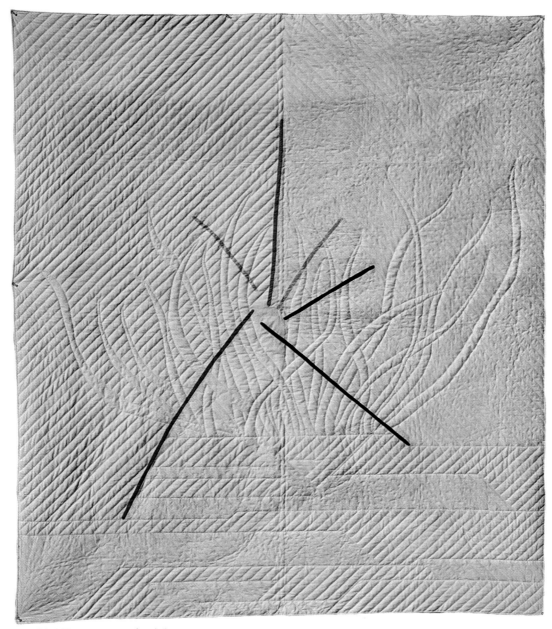

PLATE 64. Nevado del Ruiz, 82" x 86", 1986. Made by the authors.
Private Collection.
Thinking about a volcano that erupted in Columbia and killed thousands of people, we wanted to make a simple graphic representation of an exploding mountain such that every time we saw it we would be reminded of those who perished. The quilting designs were meant to represent shifting fault lines and flames.

PLATE 65. Off Center Square, 72" x 80", 1985. Made by the authors.
Inspired by an early glazed wool quilt, this is one of our "minimal" quilts that take an opposite approach to quiltmaking from that most common today. Instead of elaborate piecing and simple quilting, these are very simply pieced and elaborately quilted. The floral designs that flow through the red square are based on old patterns from bed rugs, perhaps the first blankets made in the colonies. The fantastical flowers grow from two vines, which themselves sprout from bell-shaped blossoms in the lower corners. The diagonals were marked with a long board kept aligned with angle keepers.

PLATE 66. Oriental Medallion, 84" x 84", 1981. Made by the authors.
Private Collection.

This was our second attempt at the early medallion style, with a central floral basket, *broderie perse* birds, and plain borders for fancy quilting. The feathers are oversize and thrown into relief with close diagonals, like those we have seen on early glazed wool quilts. This technique makes the feathers stand out in sharp relief.
(Photo by the authors.)

PLATE 67. Plume, 77" x 77", c.1875-1900. Maker unknown.
The quilter of this grand four-block appliqué chose to use simple echo lines, about ½"
apart. The plumes that are now white were probably once green. Though this style of
quilting has become associated with Hawaiian quilts only, it could be used with quilts
in other styles as well. Echo quilting also has the advantage of not requiring marked
lines.

PLATE 68. Rose, 64" x 76", c.1875-1900. Maker unknown.
Here is the kind of quilt we think of when we think of "classic" appliqués. The outer borders have ⅛" double diagonals ½" apart. The single diagonals inside the borders are from ¼" to ⅓" apart. Unusual feathers outline the border and form partial wreaths that are filled with very close, double, hanging diamonds. All the quilting lines run across the appliqué, instead of around it.

PLATE 69. Detail of Plate 70.

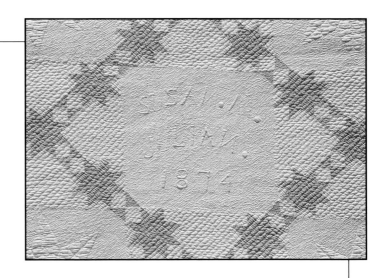

PLATE 70. Stars, 68" x 82", 1884. Made by Susan M. Julian.
We bought this quilt from a descendent of Susan M. Julian. That the maker was proud (and justifiably so) of her beautiful work shows in her trapunto signature and date in the center block. The background quilting is almost close enough to qualify as stipple quilting. The quilted stars contain small feather wreaths and feathers in each star point.

PLATE 71. Two Triangles, 68" x 75", 1985. Made by the authors.
Collection of Randy French.

In this quilt we wanted to use some of the designs of George Gardiner, the great quilt-maker from nineteenth-century Northumberland, England. The outer area has a feathered vine that seems to weave in and out of the diagonal grid. The inner quilting is taken almost exactly from a Gardiner quilt.

PLATE 72. Untitled, 82" x 82", 1989.
Made by the authors. Private Collection.

This commissioned quilt is an imitation of English "strippy" quilts, virtually the same idea as the better-known Amish Bars pattern. The quilting makes use of some classic designs from the British Isles – the split feather leaf, vines spirals, the cable – all combined in a fairly standard overall quilting layout.

PLATE 73. back, Untitled.

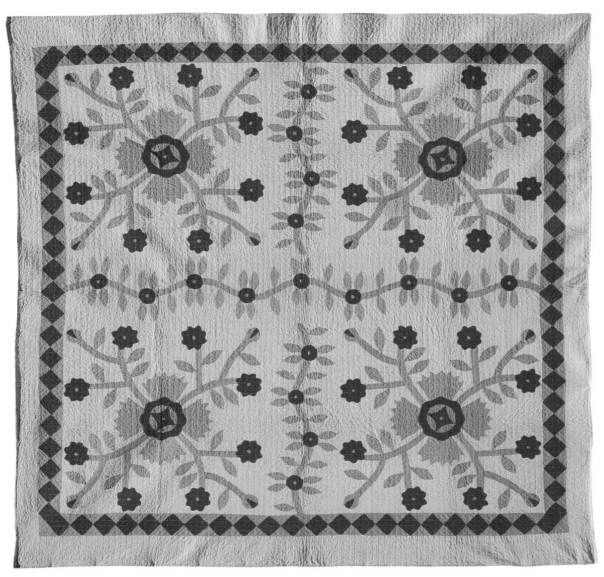

PLATE 74. Whig Rose, 84" x 84", c.1875-1900. Maker unknown.
All the appliqué, piecing and binding of this quilt was done by hand, but the quiltmaker chose to quilt the top on a treadle sewing machine, using white thread, twenty-two stitches to the inch. The grid is amazingly even and regular. We bought this quilt because it was machine quilted. We have used exactly this idea on several of our own quilts since.

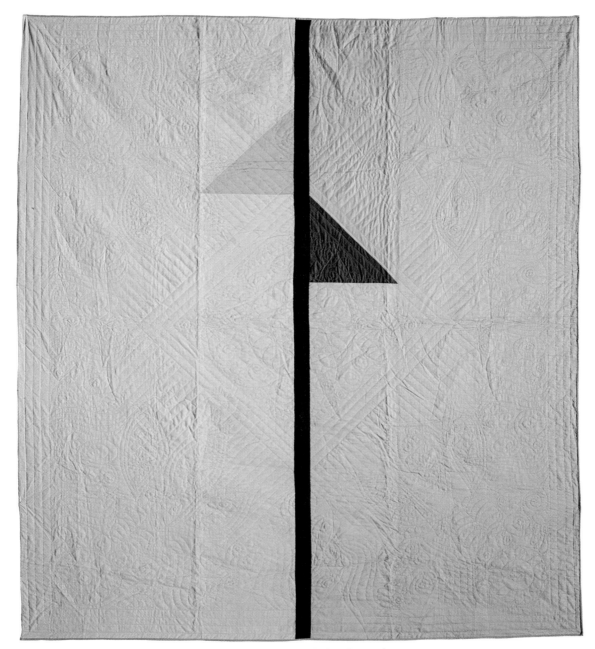

PLATE 75. Wild Goose, 71" x 87", 1984. Made by the authors.
For this highly abstracted representation of a goose on the beach we used irregular,
freely drawn versions of early English quilting designs.

GALLERY OF PATTERNS

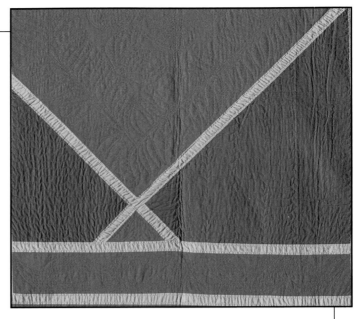

PLATE 76. Garden Island, detail. Full quilt shown page 144.

Here are some of the patterns from our collection that we have used for inspiration over the years, and a few of our own designs. Using the techniques in this book you should be able to adapt them, redraft, imitate or change them to suit your own needs.

The patterns are from various sources. First are a few from antique quilts in the collection of Mary Schafer, the great quiltmaker and collector from mid-Michigan. We transcribed the patterns by putting a piece of paper under the quilt and using a fine needle to pierce the quilting design every few stitches to make a follow-the-dot pattern on the paper.

Next are some patterns from the collection of Betty Harriman, another great quiltmaker and collector. When Betty died in 1971 Mary Schafer received all her unfinished work and patterns. Betty preferred the more ornate and

fancy designs from the last century. These have a much different effect than most modern quilting designs, partly because they are often more naturalistic.

The next three patterns are taken from cardboard templates given to Gwen by her Mennonite quilt teachers in the mid 1970's at the Zion Mennonite Church in Hubbard, Oregon.

The rest of the patterns are original designs. Included are a fullsize gothic fan pattern, and some of the patterns from the NINE PATCH quilt shown on the cover, all designed by Gwen.

Figure 324
Pattern from the Mary Schafer Collection.

Figure 325
Pattern from the Mary Schafer Collection.

Figure 326
Pattern from the Mary Schafer Collection.

Figure 327
Pattern from the Betty Harriman Collection.

Figure 328
Pattern from the Betty Harriman Collection.

Figure 329
Pattern from the Betty Harriman Collection.

Figure 330
Pattern from the Betty Harriman Collection.

Figure 331
Pattern from the Zion Mennonite Church.

Figure 332
Pattern from the Zion Mennonite Church.

Figure 333a

Pattern from the Zion Mennonite Church.

(border design)

Figure 333b

Pattern from the Zion Mennonite Church.

(corner design)

Figure 334
Pattern by the authors.

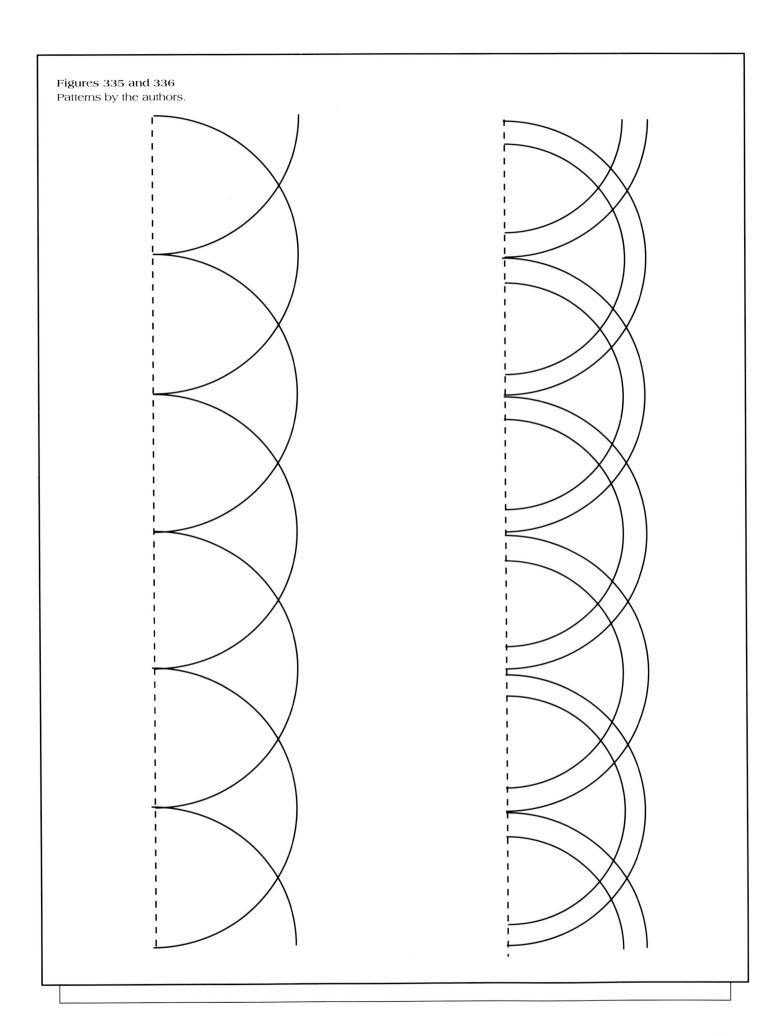

Figures 335 and 336
Patterns by the authors.

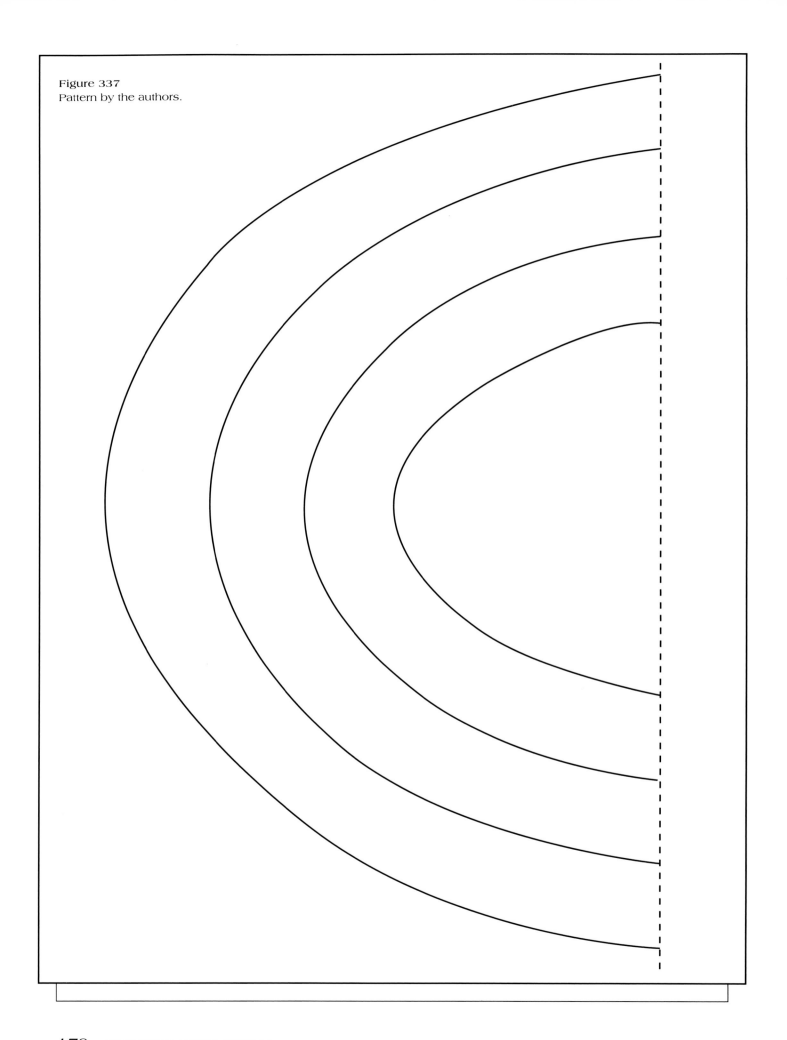

Figure 337
Pattern by the authors.

Figure 338
Pattern by Gwen Marston.

Figure 339
Pattern by Gwen Marston.

Figure 340
Pattern by Gwen Marston.

Figure 341
Pattern by Gwen Marston.

Figure 342
Pattern by Gwen Marston.

Figure 343
Pattern by Gwen Marston.

Figure 344
Pattern by Gwen Marston.

Figure 345
Pattern by Gwen Marston.

Figure 346
Pattern by Gwen Marston.

Figure 347
Pattern by Gwen Marston.

Figure 348
Pattern by Gwen Marston.

Figure 349
Pattern by Gwen Marston.

Figure 350
Pattern by Gwen Marston.

DICTIONARY OF SHAPES

BIBLIOGRAPHY

Allen, Gloria Seaman. *First Flowerings: Early Virginia Quilts*. Washington, D.C.: DAR Museum, 1987.

Bacon, Lenice Ingram. *American Patchwork Quilts*. New York: William Morrow & Co., 1973.

Bishop, Robert and Patricia Coblentz. *New Discoveries in American Quilts*. New York: E.P.Dutton and Company, 1975.

Bishop, Robert and Elizabeth Safanda. *A Gallery of Amish Quilts*. New York: E.P. Dutton and Company, 1976.

Bishop, Robert, William Secord and Judith Reiter Weissman. *Quilts, Coverlets, Rugs and Samplers*. New York: Alfred A. Knopf, 1982.

Brackman, Barbara. *American Patchwork Quilt: Quilts from the Spencer Museum*. Kokusai Art, Tokyo, Japan, 1987.

Bresenhan, Karoline and Nancy O'Bryant Puentes. *Lone Stars: A Legacy of Texas Quilts, 1836-1936*. Austin, Texas: University of Texas Press, 1986.

Bryk, Nancy Villa. *Susan McCord's Quilts*. Dearborn, Michigan: Henry Ford Museum, 1988.

Colby, Averil. *Quilting*. London: B.T. Batsford. 1972.

Curtis, Phillip H. *American Quilts in the Newark Museum Collection*. Newark, New Jersey: The Newark Museum, 1974.

Dalrymple, Marya, ed., *American Country*. Richmond, Virginia: Time-Life Books, 1989.

DeGraw, Imelda. *Quilts and Coverlets*. Denver: Denver Art Museum, 1974.

Eanes, Ellen Fickling...et.al. *North Carolina Quilts*. Chapel Hill and London: The University of North Carolina Press, 1988.

Ferrero, Pat, Elaine Hedges and Julie Silber. *Hearts and Hands*. San Francisco: The Quilt Digest Press, 1987.

Finley, Ruth E. *Old Patchwork Quilts and the Women Who Made Them*. Newton Centre, Massachusetts: Charles T. Branford Co., 1970.

Fitzrandolph, Mavis. *Traditional Quilting: Its Story and its Practice*. London: B.T. Batsford, 1954.

Fitzrandolph, Mavis, and Florence Fletcher. *Quilting*. London: Dryad Press, 1986.

Fox, Sandi. *19th Century American Patchwork Quilt*. Tokyo, Japan:
    The Seibu Museum of Art, 1983.

—————, *Small Endearments: 19th Century Quilts for Children*. New York:
    Charles Scribner's Sons, 1985.

Haders, Phyllis. *The Amish and Their Quilts*. Clinton, New Jersey:
    The Main Street Press, 1976.

Hall, Carrie A. and Rose Kretsinger. *The Romance of the Patchwork Quilt in America*.
    Coldwell, Idaho: Caxton Printers Ltd., Bonanza Books, 1935.

Havig, Bettina. *Missouri Heritage Quilts*. Paducah, Kentucky: American Quilter's Society,
    1986.

Holstein, Jonathon. *The Pieced Quilt: An American Design Tradition*. Boston:
    New York Graphic Society, 1973.

Houck, Carter and Myron Miller. *American Quilts and How to Make Them*. New York:
    Charles Scribner's Sons, 1975.

Hughes, Robert, and Julie Silber. *Amish: The Art of the Quilt*. New York: Alfred A. Knopf,
    1990.

Granick, Eve Wheatcroft. *The Amish Quilt*. Intercourse, Pennsylvania: Good Books,
    1989.

Lane, Rose Wilder. *Woman's Day Book of American Needlework*. New York:
    Simon and Schuster, 1963.

Lasansky, Jeannette. *In the Heart of Pennsylvania: 19th and 20th Century Quiltmaking
    Traditions*. Lewisburg, Pennsylvania: Oral Traditions Project, 1985.

—————, *In the Heart of Pennsylvania: Symposium Papers*. Lewisburg, Pennsylvania:
    Oral Traditions Project, 1 86.

—————, *Pieced by Mother*. Lewisburg, Pennsylvania: Oral Traditions Project, 1987.

MacDowell, Marsha, and Ruth Fitzgerald, eds. *Michican Quilts*. East Lansing, Michigan:
    Michigan State University Museum, 1987.

Marston, Gwen and Joe Cunningham. *Sets and Borders*. Paducah, Kentucky: American
    Quilter's Society, 1987.

—————, *American Beauties: Rose and Tulip Quilt*. Paducah, Kentucky:
    American Quilter's Society, 1988.

—————, *Mary Schafer and Her Quilts*. East Lansing, Michigan: Michigan State
    University Museum, 1990.

—————, *Amish Quilting Patterns*. New York: Dover Publications, 1987.

—————, *70 Classic Quilting Patterns*. New York: Dover Publications, 1987.

Nelson, Cyril, ed. *The Quilt Engagement Calender*. New York: E. P. Dutton and
    Company, 1975-1991.

Nelson, Cyril and Carter Houck. *Treasury of American Quilts*. New York: Crown Publishers, 1982.

Oliver, Celia Y., ed. *55 Famous Quilts from the Shelburne Museum*. New York: Dover Publications, 1990.

Orlovsky, Patsy and Myron. *Quilts in America*. New York: McGraw-Hill Book Company, 1974.

Osler, Dorothy. *Traditional British Quilts*. London: B.T. Batsford, 1987.

Pellman, Rachel and Kenneth Pellman. *The World of Amish Quilts*. Intercourse, Pennsylvania: Good Books, 1984.

Pottinger, David. *Quilts From the Indiana Amish*. New York: E.P. Dutton, 1983.

Quilts from Nebraska Collections. Lincoln, Nebraska: University of Nebraska, 1973.

Rae, Janet. *The Quilts of the British Isles*. New York: E.P. Dutton, 1987.

Ramsey, Bets and Marikay Waldvogel. *The Quilts of Tennessee*. Nashville, Tennessee: Rutledge Hill Press, 1986.

Safford, Carleton L. and Robert Bishop. *America's Quilts and Coverlets*. New York: E. P. Dutton and Company, Inc., 1972.

Silber, Julie. *The Esprit Quilt Collection*. San Francisco: Esprit de Corp., 1985.

Texas Heritage Quilt Society. *Texas Quilts: Texas Treasures*. Paducah, Kentucky: American Quilter's Society, 1986.

The Quilt Digest 1. San Francisco: Kiracofe and Kile, 1983.

The Quilt Digest 2. San Francisco: Kiracofe and Kile, 1984.

The Quilt Digest. San Francisco: The Quilt Digest Press, 1985.

The Quilt Digest. San Francisco: The Quilt Digest Press, 1986.

Twelker, Nancyann Johanson. *Women and Their Quilts*. Bothell, Washington: That Patchwork Place, 1988.

Walker, Michele. *The Complete Book of Quiltmaking*. New York: Alfred A. Knopf, 1986.

Webster, Marie. *Quilts: Their Story and How to Make Them*. Detroit, Michigan: The Gale Research Company, 1972. Doubleday, Page and Company, 1915.

Woodard, Thomas K. and Blanche Greenstein. *Crib Quilts and Other Small Wonders*. New York: E. P. Dutton and Company, 1981.

Index of Quilts

Other Books

by the Authors

American Beauties: Rose and Tulip Quilts, AQS, 1988.

Sets and Borders, AQS, 1987.

Amish Quilting Patterns, Dover Publications, 1987.

70 Classic Quilting Patterns, Dover Publications, 1987.

Q is for Quilt, Michigan State University Museum, 1987.

20 Little Patchwork Quilts, Dover Publications, 1990.

Mary Schafer and Her Quilts, Michigan State University Museum, 1990.

∽American Quilter's Society∽

dedicated to publishing books for today's quilters

The following AQS publications are currently available:

- **Adapting Architectural Details for Quilts,** Carol Wagner, #2282: AQS, 1991, 88 pages, softbound, $12.95
- **American Beauties: Rose & Tulip Quilts,** Gwen Marston & Joe Cunningham, #1907: AQS, 1988, 96 pages, softbound, $14.95
- **America's Pictorial Quilts,** Caron L. Mosey, #1662: AQS, 1985, 112 pages, hardbound, $19.95
- **Applique Designs: My Mother Taught Me to Sew,** Faye Anderson, #2121: AQS, 1990, 80 pages, softbound, $12.95
- **Arkansas Quilts: Arkansas Warmth,** Arkansas Quilter's Guild, Inc., #1908: AQS, 1987, 144 pages, hardbound, $24.95
- **The Art of Hand Applique,** Laura Lee Fritz, #2122: AQS, 1990, 80 pages, softbound, $14.95
- **...Ask Helen More About Quilting Designs,** Helen Squire, #2099: AQS, 1990, 54 pages, 17 x 11, spiral-bound, $14.95
- **Award-Winning Quilts & Their Makers: Vol. I, The Best of AQS Shows – 1985-1987,** #2207: AQS, 1991, 232 pages, softbound, $24.95
- **Award-Winning Quilts & Their Makers: Vol. II, The Best of AQS Shows – 1988-1989,** #2354: AQS, 1992, 176 pages, softbound, $24.95
- **Classic Basket Quilts,** Elizabeth Porter & Marianne Fons, #2208: AQS, 1991, 128 pages, softbound, $16.95
- **A Collection of Favorite Quilts,** Judy Florence, #2119: AQS, 1990, 136 pages, softbound, $18.95
- **Creative Machine Art,** Sharee Dawn Roberts, #2355: AQS, 1992, 142 pages, 9 x 9, softbound, $24.95
- **Dear Helen, Can You Tell Me?...all about quilting designs,** Helen Squire, #1820: AQS, 1987, 51 pages, 17 x 11, spiral-bound, $12.95
- **Dye Painting!,** Ann Johnston, #3399: AQS, 1992, 88 pages, softbound, $19.95
- **Dyeing & Overdyeing of Cotton Fabrics,** Judy Mercer Tescher, #2030: AQS, 1990, 54 pages, softbound, $9.95
- **Flavor Quilts for Kids to Make: Complete Instructions for Teaching Children to Dye, Decorate & Sew Quilts,** Jennifer Amor #2356: AQS, 1991, 120 pages, softbound, $12.95
- **From Basics to Binding: A Complete Guide to Making Quilts,** Karen Kay Buckley, #2381: AQS, 1992, 160 pages, softbound, $16.95
- **Fun & Fancy Machine Quiltmaking,** Lois Smith, #1982: AQS, 1989, 144 pages, softbound, $19.95
- **Gallery of American Quilts: 1849-1988,** #1938: AQS, 1988, 128 pages, softbound, $19.95
- **Gallery of American Quilts 1860-1989: Book II,** #2129: AQS, 1990, 128 pages, softbound, $19.95
- **Gallery of American Quilts 1830-1991: Book III,** #3421: AQS, 1992, 128 pages, softbound, $19.95
- **The Grand Finale: A Quilter's Guide to Finishing Projects,** Linda Denner, #1924: AQS, 1988, 96 pages, softbound, $14.95
- **Heirloom Miniatures,** Tina M. Gravatt, #2097: AQS, 1990, 64 pages, softbound, $9.95
- **Home Study Course in Quiltmaking,** Jeannie M. Spears, #2031: AQS, 1990, 240 pages, softbound, $19.95
- **Infinite Stars,** Gayle Bong, #2283: AQS, 1992, 72 pages, softbound, $12.95
- **The Ins and Outs: Perfecting the Quilting Stitch,** Patricia J. Morris, #2120: AQS, 1990, 96 pages, softbound, $9.95
- **Irish Chain Quilts: A Workbook of Irish Chains & Related Patterns,** Joyce B. Peaden, #1906: AQS, 1988, 96 pages, softbound, $14.95
- **The Log Cabin Returns to Kentucky: Quilts from the Pilgrim/Roy Collection,** Gerald Roy and Paul Pilgrim, #3329: AQS, 1992, 36 pages, 9 x 7, softbound, $12.95
- **Marbling Fabrics for Quilts: A Guide for Learning & Teaching,** Kathy Fawcett & Carol Shoaf, #2206: AQS, 1991, 72 pages, softbound, $12.95
- **More Projects and Patterns: A Second Collection of Favorite Quilts,** Judy Florence, #3330: AQS, 1992, 152 pages, softbound, $18.95
- **Nancy Crow: Quilts and Influences,** Nancy Crow, #1981: AQS, 1990, 256 pages, 9 x 12, hardcover, $29.95
- **Nancy Crow: Work in Transition,** Nancy Crow, #3331: AQS, 1992, 32 pages, 9 x 10, softbound, $12.95
- **New Jersey Quilts – 1777 to 1950: Contributions to an American Tradition,** The Heritage Quilt Project of New Jersey; text by Rachel Cochran, Rita Erickson, Natalie Hart & Barbara Schaffer, #3332: AQS, 1992, 256 pages, softbound, $29.95
- **No Dragons on My Quilt,** Jean Ray Laury with Ritva Laury & Lizabeth Laury, #2153: AQS, 1990, 52 pages, hardcover, $12.95
- **Oklahoma Heritage Quilts,** Oklahoma Quilt Heritage Project #2032: AQS, 1990, 144 pages, softbound, $19.95
- **Quilt Groups Today: Who They Are, Where They Meet, What They Do, and How to Contact Them; A Complete Guide for 1992-1993,** #3308: AQS, 1992, 336 pages, softbound, $14.95
- **Quiltmaker's Guide: Basics & Beyond,** Carol Doak, #2284: AQS, 1992, 208 pages, softbound, $19.95
- **Quilts: The Permanent Collection – MAQS,** #2257: AQS, 1991, 100 pages, 10 x 6½, softbound, $9.95
- **Scarlet Ribbons: American Indian Technique for Today's Quilters,** Helen Kelley, #1819: AQS, 1987, 104 pages, softbound, $15.95
- **Sensational Scrap Quilts,** Darra Duffy Williamson, #2357: AQS, 1992, 152 pages, softbound, $24.95
- **Sets & Borders,** Gwen Marston & Joe Cunningham, #1821: AQS, 1987, 104 pages, softbound, $14.95
- **Somewhere in Between: Quilts and Quilters of Illinois,** Rita Barrow Barber, #1790: AQS, 1986, 78 pages, softbound, $14.95
- **Stenciled Quilts for Christmas,** Marie Monteith Sturmer, #2098: AQS, 1990, 104 pages, softbound, $14.95
- **A Treasury of Quilting Designs,** Linda Goodmon Emery, #2029: AQS, 1990, 80 pages, 14 x 11, spiral-bound, $14.95

These books can be found in local bookstores and quilt shops. If you are unable to locate a title in your area, you can order by mail from AQS, P.O. Box 3290, Paducah, KY 42002-3290. Please add $1 for the first book and 40¢ for each additional one to cover postage and handling. (International orders please add $1.50 for the first book and $1 for each additional one.)